CHARLES

&

DIANA

The Royal Coat of Arms

CHARLES AND DIANA
The Prince and Princess of Wales

TEXT BY
TREVOR HALL

COLOUR LIBRARY BOOKS

Introduction

Of all the members of the Royal Family, the Sovereign alone enjoys not only a constitutional rank and dignity but also a constitutionally defined rôle. That rôle may be—indeed has been since its last major overhaul in 1689—subject to modifications, usually stealthily evolved to suit the gradual changes in our ever-developing Parliamentary democracy. It is nevertheless true, first that a number of specific constitutional functions and duties form the basis of the curriculum of the Queen's reign, and secondly that the overall residual powers vested in the monarch make her knowledge of and consent to sudden or unprecedented constitutional change an indispensable part of the process of democratic sovereignty.

The absence of regulation governing the rôles of the Queen's husband, children, mother, sister and cousins makes it difficult, to say the least, to judge how creditably each fufils the job being done. The inevitable consequence is that each rôle becomes defined according to the activities of its incumbent in performing it, with the proviso that those activities—which are public and official—and any private pursuits which are likely to come to public notice should reflect and be acceptable by reference to the social and moral levels at which the Queen's subjects conduct, or are expected to conduct, their everyday lives. Satisfying that requirement is not as easy as it sounds. On the public side, criticism lies in wait annually over the cost of the Civil List, and crops up from time to time in connection with such issues as whether one member of the Royal Family should use a helicopter during a fuel crisis when a car might do just as well, or how far a royal attendance at an Anglo-Jewish Society dinner should be counterbalanced by a similar gesture in favour of an association connected with one of the other countries involved in the delicate politics of the Middle East today. The private pursuits of the Queen's family are, because of the greater "human" interest, sometimes as public as their official activities and therefore as widely open to scrutiny and criticism. One has only to mention Gatcombe Park, blood sports, Roddy Llewellyn and the Windsors to appreciate how delicately balanced individual or collective royal reputations are, and how comprehensively the ebb and flow of public esteem affect the nation's

assessment of the suitability or efficacy of one or other royalty in the rôle into which he or she was born or married.

For the heir to the Throne, the lack of a defined rôle or of specified duties is a particularly inconvenient disadvantage. Although he enjoys a constitutional title and precedence (unlike the consort of a Queen regnant—Prince Philip's title and precedence next to the Queen exist by virtue of a Royal Proclamation and not through

A wedding has been arranged: the first official pictures of Prince Charles and Lady Diana Spencer were taken in the grounds of Buckingham Palace on the afternoon of 24th February 1981, following the announcement that morning of their engagement.

any constitutional *fiat* or convention) his life must necessarily be geared to the compulsory and continuous preparation for eventual kingship. Yet the duties of State he will ultimately be called upon to perform cannot be fully learned by experience because they are constitutionally incapable of execution by any but the reigning sovereign. It is common knowledge for instance

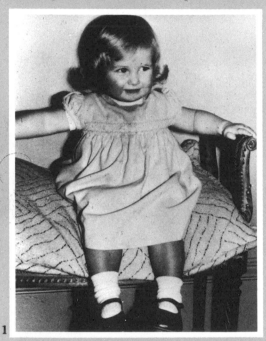

1

Early years of a future Princess of Wales: Lady Diana
Spencer *(1)* as a two-year-old, *(2)* sitting in her pram, *(3)* at the age of three—all at Park House, Sandringham, her home until 1975. *(4)* Pensive adolescence: Lady Diana on holiday on Uist in the Western Isles in the summer of 1974. *(5)* A seven-year-old Lady Diana in London in the winter of 1968.

that Queen Victoria resolutely refused to allow her eldest son to deal with, or even look at, State documents; and that King George VI at the time of his dramatic and unexpected accession in 1936 complained to his cousin Lord Louis Mountbatten that he had never seen a State paper in his life—despite the fact that for the previous quarter of a century he had been second in line to the Throne, and latterly Heir Presumptive. It follows that any heir must, if he is anxious to equip himself for his ultimate destiny, find ways of participating so closely in 2

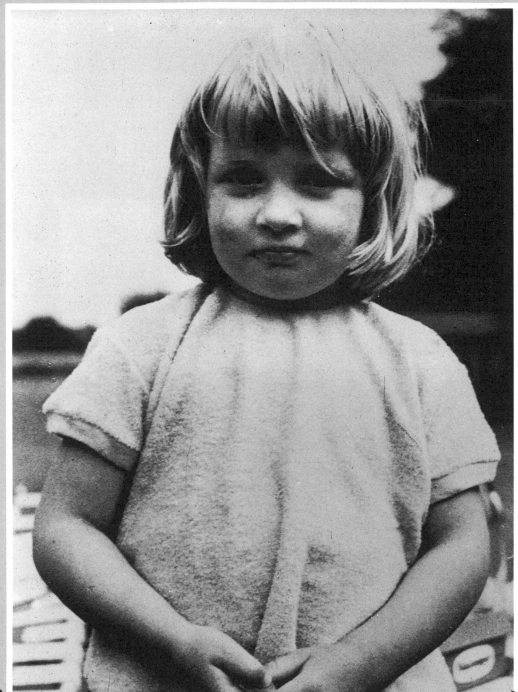

3

4

5

the affairs of State as to be able adequately to comprehend its workings, without trespassing on the prerogatives and duties of the sovereign — or indeed any other officer of State — into whose hands those affairs are constitutionally assigned.

This has not always been an easy equation to resolve. The Hanoverian period provides copi-

ous examples of heirs to the Throne making a lifetime's hobby of taking up the cudgels of the political party opposed to the one favoured by the King, and decades during which sovereigns were not on speaking terms with their eldest sons are common. In such a climate it was clearly impossible for the heir to benefit from an apprenticeship of a type which would lead to a smooth transition of constitutional power in the event of the demise of the Crown. Parental mistrust of the heir on other than political grounds — an emotion common in one degree or another to George III, Queen Victoria and George V — has also played its part in depriving Princes of Wales of the opportunity of succeeding to the Throne with the best qualifications of constitutional education and experience. The results of this recurring and unsatisfactory state of affairs have been all too obvious: the aimless extravagance of the Prince Regent coupled with

his appalling private life and his incompetence as King; the doubtful philanderings of King Edward VII throughout his forty years as Prince of Wales and the difficulty with which, as King, he genuinely strove to overcome the disadvantages of his mother's restrictions on him; the sad waste of the talents of King Edward VIII following the personal issue which, had his upbringing been a more sympathetic one and his own appreciation of constitutional issues sharper, he may never have allowed to develop to the same critical point.

It is therefore not without a sense of relief that we might look back at the very recent history of our monarchy to find that the close-knit and benign family unit which now characterises the House of Windsor has been responsible both for the trust which parent has placed in child and for the fulfilment of that trust as evidenced by the attitudes and actions of the heir, King George

(1) **Lady Diana in the grounds of the Young England** Kindergarten in September 1980. She allowed herself to be extensively photographed on this occasion *(3)*. In May of that year she had attended *(2)* the wedding of her sister Lady Sarah to Mr Neil McCorquodale. *(4)* With the Prince of Wales at Balmoral after his return from a five-week foreign tour: May 1981.

VI's proud confidence in his elder daughter—"I can, I know, always count on you to help us in our work," he wrote to her in 1947—was fully justified and rewarded by the ease with which

she deputised for him during his illnesses in 1949 and 1951, and by the assurance with which she applied herself to her duties as Queen after his untimely death in 1952. The family has stayed just as close since those eventful days, and King George's wise approach to the inevitability of the transfer of constitutional power and his sane appreciation that no-one is indispensable has clearly been adopted by his daughter in favour of Prince Charles. An official photograph, taken in 1969, exists of the Queen sitting at her desk at Windsor, one hand clutching a telephone as if she were in the midst of an important conversation. At the same time she is looking up at Prince Charles as if imparting some confidence or advice as to how it is all done. It may be

lèse-majesté to suggest that the photograph is posed, but it epitomises the spirit in which, one instinctively feels, Prince Charles' preparation for the Throne has been conducted.

The point of departure for Prince Charles was undoubtedly his Investiture as Prince of Wales in July 1969. He was still not quite out of college so that until then the public impression of him had been the nebulous one of a schoolboy at Cheam, Gordonstoun or Timbertop, or a student at Trinity College Cambridge. On St David's Day in March 1969 the image changed: as part of the run-up to the Investiture he undertook his first solo duty, and gave his first radio interview. He revealed himself as pleasantly articulate, betrayed a mature sense of humour, a love of

Keeping mum: Lady Diana politely refuses to comment on Press speculation about her friendship with Prince Charles, as photographers besiege her car: Autumn 1980 *(1, 2, 3)*. *(4)* Lonely but not alone: she makes for her car as she leaves her Knightsbridge flat for the kindergarten.

sport—he was a good swimmer, a keen skier, played cricket and polo—and a wide range of interests such as music, history, amateur dramatics and archaeology. Most of all he made it clear that he had been giving considerable thought to his future job as Prince of Wales. He had already been made a Counsellor of State (on his eighteenth birthday, 14th November 1966) so that he was eligible to deputise, with other such appointees, for the Queen during her absences abroad; he had also inaugurated his connections with Wales by taking the Chair at meetings of the planning committee responsible for "The Countryside in 1970" Conference in Cardiff, and by receiving the Freedom of the City of Cardiff —an honour accorded to his wife only three months after their marriage. He had also given notice of his dedication to the service of his country by becoming Colonel-in-Chief of the

3

Royal Regiment of Wales and by learning to fly. Within two years he was a Flight Lieutenant in the Royal Air Force, and had begun a four-year course of training and service in the Royal Navy. In 1970 he toured Australia and New Zealand with his parents, and was almost immediately afterwards off on his own, conferring independence on British colonies, attending commemorative celebrations in others, and making lengthy and significant courtesy visits to countries in all parts of the world. Now in the prime of life he is Colonel-in-Chief of over a dozen regiments, President of clubs and societies promoting everything from sub-aqua facilities to the restoration of cathedrals, Patron of associations as diverse as the Transglobe Expedition **4**

and the Welsh Association of Male Voice Choirs, and a member of about a hundred clubs ranging from the Magic Circle to the Society of Merchant Venturers. Many of these offices are of course honorary but their having been offered and accepted testifies to the scope of the Prince's interests and the energies which he is both obliged and willing to devote to them. His particular concern to be involved in schemes to help the young—the Silver Jubilee Trusts and the Prince's Trust spring to mind as obvious examples—has not only increased his wide popularity but also endowed the Crown with a greater degree of relevance to the needs and aspirations of its subjects than it might otherwise now be enjoying.

The detail of his involvement in so many areas of local and national life would command enough pages to warrant a separate book but it is enough here to assert the truth, incontrovertible on the evidence, that the Prince of Wales has formulated and established for himself a useful and productive rôle which the British Constitution confers neither by writ nor by convention, but which on the whole adequately reflects the

There is no forgetting the fact, unpalatable no doubt from his point of view, that Prince Charles' private life inevitably becomes the subject of national interest, and therefore potentially concern, in an age where privacy amongst public figures has sadly little meaning. Again we are fortunate in having a Prince of Wales whose private life has at worst been the subject of disapproval of his hunting habits and speculation —sometimes, through no fault of his own, bordering on the distasteful— as to his marriage prospects. In all other departments of his active

Lady Diana made her first appearance at Royal Ascot *(2)* **on** 16th June 1981, but did not regard hats as obligatory throughout the afternoon *(1)*. She played safe with her choice of clothes on later days *(4, 5)*. *(3)* Royal Assent: the Queen joins her son and future daughter-in-law at Buckingham Palace on 27th March where the Privy Council had just given consent to the Prince's forthcoming marriage.

interests and pursuits of an extensive cross-section of the people he will one day reign over. Furthermore it must be emphasised that, though he is constitutionally not obliged to make any exertions on behalf of anyone and could, as some of his predecessors have all too readily, adopt an existence devoted entirely to the pursuit of personal pleasure, he has seen it not only as a moral duty but also as a natural consequence of having channelled his interests for the public good in this way, to expend as much time and effort making his rôle significant and fruitful as is reasonable to expect of a person in his position.

and varied life, which should strictly speaking remain beyond public ken, he has pursued his lawful avocations with a discretion and sense of purpose from which his eagerness to impress rather than to offend may readily be inferred. That inference is strengthened by the almost constant good humour which has characterised his tolerence of the incessant and arduous pressure of public interest in him in the last dozen or so years, since he lost the protection from publicity which had previously been accorded him during his schooldays under a

1

2

convenient and well-operated arrangement between the Press and the Palace.

The subject of Prince Charles' possible marriage has probably been responsible for the greatest number of column inches devoted to any member of the Royal Family in recent years. Ever since the days of his Investiture his attachments, platonic or otherwise, to girls have been noted, reported, discussed and speculated upon with a regularity and inevitability which leaves the observer wondering why the subject was still hot news after over a decade. The answer

was probably that the more friendships he formed, the more likely it was that one of them would blossom into love—and thus marriage. For one whose public activities were so closely documented and whose private actions were always likely to be at the mercy of the legitimate or spurious interests of the photographers, Prince Charles invariably behaved with admirable forbearance while the British and foreign Press vied with each other for the best news story, obtained by fair means or foul. It is interesting to note that his patience cracked

A head for hats: both as fiancée and as wife of the Prince of Wales, Lady Diana sported a plucky line in headwear: bonnets at Ascot in June *(1, 2, 4)* and wide brims *(3)* in North Wales in October.

only when the liaison which came under close Press scrutiny was that involving his final courtship—with Lady Diana Spencer. In November 1980 he became openly testy with photographers and film cameramen during a polo match in India, and the following January, unable to discourage them from beseiging the Royal Family on their pheasant shoots at Sand-

ringham, he voiced the Queen's displeasure as well as his own in terms so unusually vitriolic that it set Fleet Street editors seriously rethinking their attitudes. Fortunately for everyone the immediate conflict of interests did not last long enough to develop into anything resembling a major problem. Within just over a month the Prince of Wales' engagement to Lady Diana was announced and the opportunities for public discussion and legitimate photography of the couple together improved immediately.

At that point of her engagement it was perhaps an advantage to Lady Diana that the rôle of Princess of Wales is as lacking in definition as that of a Prince of Wales. It meant at least that there was no immediate necessity for her to be trained up to any rigidly specified standard—something which would have been

4

impossible and manifestly undesirable in the time available—before her duties as wife of the heir to the Throne could begin. Nevertheless, as Prince Charles anticipated more than a decade before, the advantage of marrying a girl who is *already* a princess is that she knows what to do and how to go about performing royal duties, whereas a commoner does not have this useful

3

1

2

Talk of the town: Lady Diana at Goldsmiths Hall in March *(1),* and Lord Snowdon's official portrait of her, taken around the same time *(2). (3)* Lady Diana arrives at the Victoria and Albert Museum for the "Splendours of the Gonzaga" exhibition in November. *(4)* Qualified enthusiasm: watching, with bated breath, Prince Charles playing polo at Windsor in June.

head start. It was therefore imperative that Lady Diana should lose no time in being schooled in that art forthwith, and bearing in mind that she would be understandably preoccupied with the preparations, both physical and psychological, for the supreme national event which was to be her wedding, it might seem with hindsight that her introduction to what Prince Charles had already warned her were the awful necessities of royal life was almost cruelly swift and relentless.

For, despite his appreciation of the difficulties, Prince Charles could not have chosen for his wife a less public figure than Lady Diana. Although she was the daughter of an Earl, her upbringing had been nothing if not homely and her early years were devoid of encounters which might have brought her any kind of publicity. The very public and hard-fought divorce proceedings between her parents in 1969 carried the family name willy-nilly into the headlines but far from blooding Lady Diana— then only eight-years-old—to cope with exposure of this kind, it seems only to have encouraged her to retreat into her shell as she pursued her unspectacular educational career, through two changes of school, to its eventual

3

conclusion. A brief interlude at a finishing school in Switzerland and the beginning of what might have been a long vocation at the Young England Kindergarten in Pimlico saw her almost to the end of her essentially private first twenty years, before she made undoubtedly the most dramatic decision in personal terms that any girl of that age could be called upon to consider. The *Morning Star* churlishly interpreted that decision in the most derogatory way possible, accusing Lady Diana of giving up her independence for the sake of "a few lousy foreign holidays." What combination of factors— prestige, love, ambition, sense of duty— impelled her to agree to marry Prince Charles it will **4**

undoubtedly be many years—if ever— before we really know, but as soon as the official announcement of the engagement was made her private life ended for ever, and her first job was to get used to the radical changes of life-style which her prestigious decision entailed.

The most immediate changes were obvious: the day after the engagement all Lady Diana's belongings were removed from the Knightsbridge flat which she had until then shared with three other girls (who turned out to be as loyal and discreet as she could have wished) and taken to Clarence House where she immediately took up residence with the Queen Mother. At the same time her employment at the kindergarten came to an end: no more would she travel daily

2

3

To the church on time: *(1)* **Lady Diana Spencer leaves** Clarence House for St Paul's in the Glass Coach on her wedding day, 29th July 1981. *(2)* Pride and confidence with *Pomp and Circumstance*, as the Prince and his bride walk down the aisle after their marriage. *(3)* Their joyful return to Buckingham Palace.

to and from that modest school building and be called "Miss Diana." The smart red Mini Metro car in which she had made those now famous journeys, whether pursued by paparazzi or not, was forsaken—and eventually sold back to British Leyland—in favour of the official limousines which for decades have transported royalty gracefully and effortlessly from place to place. Lady Diana had additionally to accustom herself to being shadowed by a personal dectective wherever she went, and protected by policemen surrounding every building she might occupy or visit. There were the instant necessities of arranging for dresses to be made to suit all occasions, State and official, in which both as the fiancée and later as the wife of the Prince of Wales she would be required to participate. Official photographs, some to commemorate the engagement and others for issue on the eve of their marriage, had to be taken, and Lord Snowdon who had already photographed Lady Diana the previous year was now favoured with a multiple assignment comprising both formal and informal pictures of the couple, and including the classic studies of them at Highgrove— Prince Charles wearing naval uniform and his fiancée in evening dress.

Unlike most engaged young ladies, Lady Diana faced the problem of protocol over the title by which she would be known after her marriage. It caused some surprise when the Palace announced that "The Princess of Wales" and "Diana Princess of Wales" would be acceptable but that "Princess Diana" would not. This was evidently because she would be a Princess only by marriage and not in her own right, so that if she were to be called "Princess" anything, she would have to take her husband's name and be called "Princess Charles." This, the Palace admitted, might sound strange, but it did accord

with the rule under which Princess Richard of Gloucester was, and Princess Michael of Kent is now, styled—and people would get used to it in due course. In the event the appellation "Princess Charles" has never been used, and those sections of the Press and publishing world seeking a more informal term than "Princess of Wales" preferred to ignore the Palace's diktat and referred to her as Princess Diana, or more familiarly Princess Di.

These novelties fundamental though they

(1) **Together before God: the Archbishop of Canterbury gives** divine blessing on the Prince and Princess of Wales. *(2)* Together before the Queen: the customary gesture of homage from the bride and groom. *(3)* Together before the people: a famous balcony kiss which seals the union.

were, exercised Lady Diana's ability to adapt less formidably than some of the more subtle changes with which she was about to have to cope. One of these was that, as a potential new member of the nation's first family, her private actions and emotions were, rightly or wrongly, more likely to become public property than before. Her past life was already being researched in such depth that any newsworthy details would without doubt have been extensively noised abroad, and she now knew that her every expression, comment and gesture would

call for the greatest discretion, and that all her likes and dislikes would be systematically recorded in word or picture at the earliest opportunity and without so much as a by your leave. For it is a fact which the Royal Family, like most public figures, have now learned to live with that those who are accorded a place in the news because of their rank or success remain potential news material twenty-four hours a day, and the intrusive flash of the camera and click of the tape-recorder are as much a part of their existence as the very act of breathing. This of course was something which Lady Diana learned in those late Summer weeks of 1980, but she now bore the added responsibility of being more than the Prince of Wales' girlfriend: shortly to join the Royal Family itself, she well appreciated that her behaviour would become part of the royal "image" every bit as much as the well-known mannerisms of any of the established members of that Family. Fortunately the indomitable discretion she had displayed before her engagement continued throughout 1981, and for the most part reporters avid for evidence of default were disappointed. The only occasions when the private emotions of Lady Diana got the better of her occurred at the end of March when she broke down as she watched her fiancé take off for his five-week tour of Australia and New Zealand, and again at Smith's Lawn Windsor during the final weekend before her wedding when the anticipation of the days to come, the stress of watching Prince Charles playing polo —a sight she clearly does not relish—and the strain of coping with the incessant crush of photographers who followed her everywhere at close quarters, forced her to leave the field in floods of tears. All things considered, it was not a bad record, but it was telling that the Queen took the matter firmly in hand the following December when Press interest in the now pregnant Princess became insatiable and furtive. Following the publication of pictures showing her giving Prince Charles a spontaneous hug in a private moment at Highgrove House, editors were called to Buckingham Palace. There they were told of the Queen's concern that the Princess was being dogged by photographers everywhere, and that at a time when she should be subject to the least possible strain the clear duty of the Press was to reduce their intrusion on her private life to a minimum. There could be **1**

little doubt that this reaction was prompted by the memory of that regrettable incident at Windsor the previous July and by anxiety that it should not be repeated.

Closely associated with the need to cope with her own "news value" was the paramount necessity of attaching the proper degree of credibility—or even a mere attention—to public criticism and the breath of scandal. Public criticism of the sovereign and members of the Royal Family is of course nothing new, but history shows that it comes and goes into and out of fashion, and that the most recent passion for taking pot-shots at royalty wholesale began about twenty-five years ago. In those days it was people like Lord Altrincham, Kingsley Martin and Malcolm Muggeridge who wrote detailed and usually logically-argued articles touching upon the suitability of the monarchy as an institutional part of our Parliamentary democracy, the system of privilege which surrounds it and which it helps to perpetuate, and the style in which the Palace (to use a respectfully safe and vague term) operates the institution itself. Discussion of this kind is freer than it was—the whole concept of criticism is more widely tolerated—but the tendency has been for a degree of pettiness to enter into the complaints written or spoken by the Press or members of the public. Such complaints may now centre around the Queen's choice of clothes, the Duke of Edinburgh's choice of language, Prince Charles' choice of sports, Princess Anne's choice of a home or Princess Margaret's choice of a companion. In the comparatively short time during which she has been subjected to it the Princess of Wales has taken her fair share of this brand of criticism on the chin. Her first official outing in what has been boringly termed THAT dress drew howls of incredulity that she should dare wear anything so immodest on her début, though in private as in public many admired her sense of adventure. Some commentators used this as an excuse to scrutinise all her wardrobe for evidence of attempts to up-stage the Queen on the few occasions when both were present at the same time. There were more general reac-

The Princess waving triumphantly (1) in response to the thunderous roar of the crowds outside St Paul's, before descending the red-carpeted steps with the Prince (2) towards the waiting carriage.

2

tions to her choice of fashion which at times almost divided the nation. Some found her frills and ornate hats too fussy while others were delighted that she had no hesitation in sporting a line very much her own. More recently, and more seriously, she has been severly criticised for allegedly taking part in blood sports at Balmoral and a particularly virulent castigation

Above: **a moment to savour at the door of St Paul's.**
Left: a private word between man and wife before they enter the carriage for the journey back to the Palace. *Right:* Lichfield's official photograph of the couple.

by the League Against Cruel Sports was bolstered by a graphic report that she had attended the disembowelling of a stag. She was also reported, not long after she and Prince Charles returned to Balmoral after their honeymoon abroad, as dissatisfied and disillusioned with the life-style there: the detail of the allegation was clear enough to endow it with a short-lived credibility and to cause considerable distress to the Princess. However well she disguised or threw off that distress in the ensuing weeks when all eyes were upon her as she embarked upon her pubic career, she will appreciate that criticism, justified or unwarranted, trivial or major, is ready to spring up with every public or private move she makes.

The news in November of her pregnancy may well have been instrumental in keeping potential critics at bay: insofar as the Press instigates or purveys sensations about members of the Royal Family the commercially exploitable human interest in the Princess' approaching confinement was far too great to be endangered by anything stronger than well-meant advice or

(1) A quick word: Prince Charles and his bride in St Paul's.
(2) A long walk: newly married, they face their wedding guests.
(3) A happy wave: an exultant Prince and Princess acknowledge the cheering crowds.

the occasional routine gripe. Indeed the announcement itself, coming, it seemed, hard on the heels of the wedding, brought the Princess to the peak of her popularity, while the significance of the pregnancy, heralding the arrival of possibly the next monarch but one made her the protégée of the nation. She was not, even at twenty years of age, the youngest Princess of Wales to have been expecting a baby—Princess Alexandra, consort of the future King Edward VII was only just eighteen when her first child was expected. Nor was the apparent swiftness of the conception more than commonplace in the historical pattern of royal

births—in the whole of the last three centuries King George II and King George VI have been the only sovereigns since Queen Anne not to have produced their eldest children within a year of their marriages. But somehow the Princess of Wales' youth coupled with the comparative surprise with which the news of her pregnancy was received, enhanced the great supportive following which she had already done much to secure. Few are the souls who will not observe her progress with at least a degree of interest and goodwill.

Although the weeks immediately following the news of her condition were blighted by morning sickness which obliged her to cancel many engagements until quite shortly before Christmas 1981, it was cheering to learn that the resumption of her duties in December would continue until early April. It would have been a great dissapointment if, however understandable the reason for it, her timetable had been completely abandoned until well after the birth of her baby: in that event she would by then have been in the unusual position, over a year after her marriage, of being better known to the country as the Prince of Wales' fiancée than as his wife. This odd situation will fortunately not now arise and the current arrangements will give the royal couple the opportunity to gauge how far the exercise of their public duties is compatible with the pursuit of their private happiness, and to decide how to accomplish both without prejudicing either.

For in carving out and moulding their life together in a manner which achieves the best mix, the Prince and Princess of Wales will not be able to look reliably on precedent or guidance. The Prince's parents, who were the last—indeed the only—post-War members of the Royal Family to experience the same degree of proximity to the Throne, were in 1947 almost immediately alerted to the distressing probability that they would be called upon at short notice to assume the trappings of sovereignty, and much of their early married life consisted of successive major duties delegated to them by the ailing King George VI. Prince Charles and his wife face no such awesome prospect: the

(1) **Members of the wedding: the Prince and Princess of Wales** with their supporters, bridesmaids and pages. *(2)* The Princess in her magnificent wedding dress. **2**

Queen is in the best of health, has already passed the age at which her father died, and happily shows no intention of acceding to the thinly-veiled suggestions, submitted at regular and frequent intervals over the last three years, that she should abdicate in favour of her eldest son. Those recommendations may well be resurrected once the Princess of Wales' baby is born, but they are unlikely to be heeded. The signs are that both the Prince and Princess will wish to spend a considerable time away from the heavy round of public duties which await them to enjoy and consolidate their family—and who would deny this to a man who, a bachelor for nearly thirty-three years, has chosen his wife and our future Queen with impeccable aptitude, or to a young woman who, ever since she first came to public attention, has made no secret of her love and concern for young children?

Of course the demands of their station will call them both away from the private enjoyment of their home and family at Highgrove: already the Princess' pregnancy has caused the postponement of trips to Australia, New Zealand and Canada which had been promised for 1982, and these obligations which, in the case of the former two countries at least, Prince Charles has vowed will be honoured, will remain to be fufilled after the baby's birth. In addition there will be invitations for them to visit countries throughout the world as well as the clamour from those parts of the British Isles where potential hosts have hoped so far in vain for the chance to entertain the Prince and his popular wife. If the rumours about the Princess' wish for a substantial family are true, the balance between the discharge of her public obligations and her own personal fulfilment as a wife and mother is likely to be achieved and maintained only with considerable effort.

The style in which the couple will carry out their duties together prompts further speculation. Despite the imaginative inauguration of the royal walk-about—a public relations device first applied by the Queen and Prince Philip in Australia and New Zealand in 1970 as an antidote to the sort of reception, rather sullen and indifferent, which they were surprised to have been accorded during their previous tour there in 1963—most senior members of the Royal Family have kept their distance from the common herd who loyally turn out through rain and shine to see and greet them. The select or lucky few have been able to exchange a few words with a royal visitor; children have, particularly on festive occasions, been allowed to run up and present gifts and bouquets of flowers. But on the whole the ever-present security requirements, the demands of time-keeping, the fear of the untoward or embarrassing incident and, it must be admitted, a certain natural aloofness have over the years combined to deprive even an informal walkabout of much of its intended spontaneity and originality.

Prince Charles is without doubt one of the less staid interpreters of the rules of meeting people. In his time he has developed a noticeably easy and fluid style which prompts him to dive into crowds, shake hands with all and sundry, and prolong conversations when the subject matter is of genuine interest to him. He is game for anything at almost any time, and has impressed his public with his unrehearsed readiness to skate-board, shear sheep, ride camels or join in vigorous disco or folk dances, as much as by the more organised pursuits of parachuting, windsurfing, horseriding and rifle-shooting. His soubriquet of Clown Prince may well be an undesirable cliché but it proclaims his innate and lasting sense of good fun and his willingness to exercise it in public—at least to the extent just short of which extreme formality would render it unsuitable. In the same way the Princess of Wales gave early notice of her essentially natural informality of manner, and of her determination (if indeed there was ever any question of making an active decision about it)

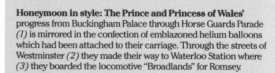

Honeymoon in style: The Prince and Princess of Wales' progress from Buckingham Palace through Horse Guards Parade *(1)* is mirrored in the confection of emblazoned helium balloons which had been attached to their carriage. Through the streets of Westminster *(2)* they made their way to Waterloo Station where *(3)* they boarded the locomotive "Broadlands" for Romsey.

to allow it to pervade the performance of her public duties. Her encounters with her future subjects, right from that first visit to Cheltenham in March 1981, have been littered with incidents which even a few years ago would have been almost unthinkable. Her contact with people has been tactile as well as merely visual; she has kissed and been kissed; she has chatted at length and in a lively and interested way; she has swapped jokes with her husband in public; she has twitted pressmen, cradled babies, cuddled toddlers and enjoyed the company and conversation of children generally. This delightful and popular approach was reaffirmed with particular success during the momentous three-day tour of Wales which the Prince and Princess made the springboard of their official life together, and hundreds of children and adults alike who unexpectedly became the enthralled recipients of her imaginative attentions will each remember those few special moments for ever.

The evolution of rôles for a modern-day Prince and Princess of Wales has thus begun fittingly, and the manner in which those rôles are being played augurs well for the future of our monarchy. The spirit of rededication which permeated the splendours of the Royal Wedding celebrations lives on in the Royal Family, where the rising young generation waits to make its own distinctive mark on the future development of a nation liable to become periodically impatient of empty tradition and stagnation. The valuable experience and indeed expertise of Prince Charles combined with his wife's refreshingly innovative flair will prove of immense significance as the British monarchy, which at times few would have expected to outlive the twentieth century, sails confidently into the twenty-first. We may justly hope that, when in that century the times comes, the couple who will have done much to sustain the Crown's influence and popularity will, as King and Queen, reap the benefits of their efforts.

A smiling Princess of Wales, wearing a drop-pearl tiara, riding to the Palace of Westminster to attend for the first time the State Opening of Parliament by the Queen. The following day an an even happier event was announced!

CHARLES & DIANA
The Prince & Princess of Wales

The Lord Mayor of London put it in a nutshell, and beautifully. Speaking only two hours after the official announcement that Diana, Princess of Wales was expecting a baby, he likened the memory of her recent marriage to Prince Charles to "the everlasting lustre of a gold ingot," and continued: "a gold ingot that has now been supremely hallmarked by this morning's announcement that Your Royal Highnesses are to be blessed with a child, for which we all rejoice."

• It was 5th November 1981, and the Prince and Princess were attending a luncheon at the Guildhall held to mark the City of London's appreciation of what it rightly regarded as the sublime favour of having held their wedding ceremony at St Paul's Cathedral, within the City's bounds. The news of the Princess' pregnancy was of course known to all the guests gathered for the occasion but this happy reference to it by Sir Ronald Gardner-Thorpe at one of his last functions as Lord Mayor of London gave them all the opportunity to respond with warm, sincere and prolonged applause. Prince Charles looked around him with evident satisfaction; his wife, less used to having her personal news mentioned or discussed on grandiose occasions, was unable to restrain a smile, but nevertheless bowed her head and blushed modestly.

As well she might, for quite apart from her own personal joy of prospective motherhood, this 20-year-old Princess was now the centre of the world's attention as possibly the mother of a future sovereign of the United Kingdom of Great Britain and Northern Ireland. The prospect has, of course, to be hedged with reservations: the child now expected might be a girl, and liable to be nudged further down the line of succession by any future male child born to the

Princess. Even a male child's succession could not be guaranteed, as the fairly recent history of the Royal Family shows. Only 45 years ago, King Edward VIII, though he actually became King, was obliged to abdicate before his Coronation, bringing his younger brother to the Throne as King George VI. And less than 45 years before that, Prince Albert Victor—who, as the Princess of Wales's expected baby will be, was heir to the Throne directly after his father—died suddenly at the age of 28 so that *his* younger brother became heir in his place and finally succeeded as King George V. With the present Queen in only her 56th year, the uncharted and sometimes devious path of fate makes it impossible to suppose with any certainty what the ultimate status of 1982's royal baby will be. All that can be predicted with reasonable accuracy is that, no matter what its sex, he or she will at birth be second in line to the Throne of a thousand years and will thus be invested with the aura, mystique, private care and public attention which has for centuries been the fate of all royal babies of similar rank.

For the Princess of Wales, to whom, with her special affection for young children, the birth and upbringing of her first child will give the greatest possible pleasure, the awesome prospect of bringing into the world a baby destined for kingship or a position close to it must have seemed an impossibly far cry from the carefree days just over a year before when, as Lady Diana Spencer, she was one of four girls sharing a flat (admittedly comparatively capacious) in Knightsbridge as a pied-à-terre during her employment as a kindergarten schoolteacher in Pimlico, and with no special claim to public attention or fame. True, she was the daughter of an Earl, but the youngest daughter at that; and with a brother Charles, Viscount Althorp,

who would in any event succeed to the Earldom, she was certainly no heiress. Both of her elder sisters had married—Lady Sarah to Mr Neil McCorquodale and Lady Jane to Mr Robert Fellowes, who is an assistant private secretary to the Queen—and in a way Lady Diana, perhaps without realising it and certainly without resenting it, was the Cinderella of the family.

But the makings of a royal connection existed. Quite apart from the many historical links with royalty, dating back to King Charles II and probably beyond, her father, the 8th Earl, had been equerry to King George VI and to the present Queen between 1950 and 1954; her maternal grandmother Ruth, Lady Fermoy, is a lady-in-waiting to the Queen Mother; Viscount Althorp is a godson of the Queen and, because of the close personal friendships which have blossomed between the Royal Family and the Spencers (who, until 1975 when Lord Spencer inherited the Earldom, lived in Park House, a tenanted dwelling on the Sandringham estate) various members, past and present of the British Royal Family have attended the weddings, christenings and memorial services of the Spencer clan.

It was thus inevitable that the Queen's children and the Spencer offspring should have known each other tolerably well during early childhood and adolescence alike, and for that reason alone it is difficult to identify the precise occasion when Lady Diana and Prince Charles "first met." It seems fairly common ground, particularly as it has now been publicly confirmed by the Prince, that the first meeting at which eyes began to twinkle occurred in November 1977 when the 29-year-old heir to the Throne was a guest at the Spencer's imposing family seat at Althorp in Northamptonshire. At

that time, Prince Charles' name was being romantically linked with that of Lady Diana's sister Sarah, and it was indeed she whom he took with him to the Swiss resort of Klosters the following January for his annual ski-ing holiday. But Lady Diana also took his eye: he found her

"a splendid 16-year-old" and full of fun, and when almost three years later, (long after his close relationship with Lady Sarah had, like several subsequent friendships, passed), Lady Diana appeared at Balmoral for a short holiday, he resumed his once fleeting attention for her. This meeting at Balmoral was coincidental in that Lady Diana's sister Jane, necessarily attached to the Queen's private household that summer through her husband's position there, was having a baby. The footloose Lady Diana, her school term over, came up to help. That was in July 1980, and less than two months later, the Prince arranged further meetings, complete with several ploys designed to throw the ever-threatening Press off the scent. For one such meeting, Lady Diana travelled to Scotland ostensibly to stay with the Queen Mother at

Birkhall where, though close to Balmoral, she was unlikely to be traced or spotted. During that visit the couple spent many days together walking, picnicking and fishing, and gradually warming to the realisation that, as Prince Charles rather shyly put it later, "there was

Above, a peep at the photographers. *Opposite,* a more leisurely pose in the kindergarten grounds in September, 1980.

something in it." It was not very long after Lady Diana's return to London for the new school term that she and her admirer realised that their budding romance had not gone unnoticed. The newspapers were suddenly full of speculative sensation about their relationship, prompted by the publication of a rather blurred photograph purporting to be of the couple fishing on the River Dee. Within the next twenty-four hours the world's Press had beaten a path to Lady Diana's flat and another one to the kindergarten where she thenceforth continued against all odds to pursue her chosen vocation.

Her attempt to do so was more easily em-

barked upon than persevered with, for the more widespread the news became, the more clamorous became the demands made upon her. Hounded each morning from the first step she took from her flat to the last mad dash from her car to the school buildings, and facing the perpetually daunting prospect of similar treatment on the return journey, Lady Diana's life became a daily ordeal in which, quite unable to dodge public attention, she had to draw upon vast reserves of diplomacy, tact and patience almost unthinkable in a mere 19-year-old. To the surprise and admiration of everyone, however, she developed those very attributes to the extent that within a very short time her pursuers knew exactly how far to go. She allowed herself to be photographed outdoors whilst remaining firmly tight-lipped against all personal questions—so much so that the time came when she was hardly news any longer. By that time her mother, Mrs Frances Shand Kydd (the first wife of Earl Spencer and divorced from him in 1969) had complained bitterly to the Press about the treatment to which her daughter was being subjected and many editors called off the chase. But at various intervals thereafter—particularly in mid-November when Prince Charles invited Lady Diana to Sandringham to spend the weekend of his 33rd birthday, the Press, both British and foreign, had guessed, probably rightly, that he at least had made up his own mind that she would be his future wife, and they consequently resurrected their professional interest in the couple.

Like his mother before him, Prince Charles had to endure a considerable absence from the object of his affections. In his case there was a tour of India and Nepal to carry out in late November and December of 1980. In the case of the then Princess Elizabeth in 1947, her prospective engagement was deliberately delayed so that she could join the Royal Family on the South African tour of that year, and probably so that she could use the enforced absence from her future fiancé to reflect on the merits of her decision. "I am so glad," wrote her father, King George VI, to her after her wedding, "that you wrote and told Mummy that you think the long wait before your engagement . . . was for the best. I was afraid you had thought I was being rather hard-hearted about it." Prince Charles,

however, was subject to no such parental restriction since the Indian tour had been planned long before Lady Diana came onto the scene: he would have wished to go in any event, both because of his desire to see the country with such strong connections with his beloved great-uncle, Lord Mountbatten, and because of the opportunity it would give him to visit, for the first time since 1975, his great friend King Birendra of Nepal.

After a colourful and successful tour, Prince Charles was back in time to celebrate Christmas with his family at Windsor, and the New Year at Sandringham. News filtered through that Lady Diana would be joining him again at Sandringham and another flood of reporters and photographers invaded the roads surrounding the extensive private estate in order to catch a glimpse of her. Fortunately, a more experienced Palace personnel was able to protect her from the intrusive glare of publicity, and the closest the Press got to real hard news was represented by a feast of photographs of almost everyone at Sandringham *except* Lady Diana, and a fierce and uncharacteristically malevolent blast of opprobrium from Prince Charles who wished reporters "a happy New Year and your editors a particularly nasty one."

It was shortly after this—few, if any, outside the royal circle know quite when—that the Prince proposed to his lady and was accepted. He later confessed himself "frankly amazed that she should want to take me on" and, knowing more than most about the disadvantages of royal life, suggested that she should take time freely to consider all the implications of her decision: "I wanted to give her time," he said, "to consider whether it was all going to be too awful." She therefore journeyed, as planned, to stay with her mother in Australia for a month, where she duly reflected on the prospects of being Princess of Wales—prospects from which, as was said of Queen Victoria's task at her accession, an archangel might well shrink—and from where she telephoned the Prince to confirm her belief that she could

Opposite, **Lady Diana maintains a tight-lipped diplomacy** against the persistent questions of reporters outside her flat; September, 1980. *This page,* time to relax as schoolboy Nicholas Hardy offers his "future Queen" a daffodil and his homage at Cheltenham on 27th March, 1981.

shoulder the responsibilities as well as enjoy the privileges that her life as the wife of the heir to the Throne would involve.

The engagement was concluded at that time, but Britain was obliged to await news of it. When ultimately Lady Diana returned from Australia—on Prince Andrew's 21st birthday—there was little immediate knowledge of her arrival: indeed it was with some surprise that people learned she had not only returned, but was immediately with Prince Charles when on the following day his National Hunt horse Allibar collapsed and died after a training gallop at the Lambourn stables of Nick Gaselee.

The consequent disclosure of their continuing close relationship could well have been the catalyst for the official announcement of their engagement which came at 11 o'clock on the morning of 24th February: "It is with the greatest of pleasure that the Queen and the Duke of Edinburgh announce the betrothal of their beloved son the Prince of Wales to the Lady Diana Spencer, daughter of the Earl Spencer and the Hon Mrs Shand Kydd."

So ended the demanding and difficult saga of

how a Prince of Wales woos and wins his lady in modern times. It compares appallingly, from the participants' point of view, with the discreet and respectful manner in which such procedures were accomplished even as recently as the immediate post-war period. But the British monarchy has since then learned to live and indeed cope with the potential intrusions into the private lives of its members, inevitable consequences of the publicity machine which records relentless details of its public activities as a matter of course. It must be said that both Prince Charles, who has tolerated over a decade of speculation about his possible marriage partner, and Lady Diana who, thirteen years his junior, endured her baptism by fire with consummate good grace, had both proved

themselves equal to even some of the worst excesses of public exposure at a time of the most intense personal pressure.

For Lady Diana, the ordeal of entry into public life was only just beginning. Being other than royalty herself, she did not have the advantage enjoyed by the majority of her predecessors of knowing precisely and in detail what to do and how to conduct herself according to royal precedent when in the public eye. Her initiation into the ways of royalty had therefore to begin immediately. There was time for a private visit to Cholmondeley, the Cheshire home of the Duke of Westminster, the weekend following the engagement and for a private evening at the Covent Garden Opera on 3rd March, before the first official function attended by Lady Diana was arranged. It was from all points of view a stunning success.

The occasion, now well imprinted on the minds of those who saw its reporting, was a recital of music at Goldsmiths Hall London, in aid of the Royal Opera House Development Appeal, of which the Prince is Patron. The crowd which gathered outside in the pouring rain for a brief glimpse of the future Princess were well rewarded when she arrived in what was politely described as an off-the-shoulder gown: it was in effect probably the most revealing dress ever worn even by any well-

Opposite page and above, four hours after the official announcement of their engagement on 24th February, 1981, Prince Charles and his fiancée were photographed at Buckingham Palace. Their secret revealed, Lady Diana looked considerably more at ease than during the previous months of speculation, *right.*

established member of the Royal Family, let alone by the fiancée of a Prince of Wales on her very first public outing. It was designed for her by the small London partnership Emanuels, run by husband and wife David and Liz Emanuel, whom Lady Diana had already chosen to design

Right and below, **a family** occasion with a difference. Prince Charles took Lady Diana to Broadlands, the Hampshire home of the late Lord Mountbatten, to open a large exhibition on 9th May, 1981. After the official ceremony, the couple went into the extensive grounds to plant two saplings commemorating their visit. Then, clutching posies of flowers thrust into her hands by spectators, Lady Diana joined the Prince on a walkabout, *far right and opposite.*

her wedding dress. This foretaste of daring innovation rocketed the couple to instant fame.

The following week, Lady Diana was introduced to the protocol of the State occasion when she attended a banquet given by the Queen for the President of Nigeria, then on a State Visit to Britain. She then spent "a lovely weekend" at snow-covered Balmoral where she and the Prince took long walks and fished together at the Queen Mother's stretch of salmon-fishing water on the River Dee. Soon she was back in the public gaze again as the Queen held a Privy Council at which formal approval was given to the Prince's forthcoming marriage. Immediately after that Council Lady Diana and Prince

As the photographs overleaf show, Lady Diana preferred to spend her time with children. The spontaneous greeting, the jokes enjoyed by all, the toddlers picked up and cuddled, the gifts and flowers readily accepted, the little confidences shared between the eminent visitor and her young admirers...all were examples of Lady Diana's winning brand of informality which helped to make her instantly and universally popular in the early weeks of her engagement.

Charles were photographed officially with the Queen for the first time: Prince Philip could not be included in the picture because he was in Australia at the time. That afternoon the Prince and his fiancée went down to Cheltenham where, anticipating their ultimate move to Highgrove House, recently purchased by the Prince, they visited the headquarters of the Gloucestershire Constabulary, whose job it would be to ensure the security of the mansion. During that visit Lady Diana was gallantly accosted by a 17-year-old schoolboy, Nicholas Hardy, who presented her with a daffodil and asked to "kiss the hand of my future Queen." Reports of Lady Diana's reaction are conflict-

ing: according to one she said "Well, I don't know about that," while another report quoted her as accepting gleefully. Whatever the truth of it, she did allow herself to be kissed in this way, and there was national delight when the photographs were published the next day to prove it. It gave, above all, an indication that

here was someone with a fresh approach to the task of undertaking royal duties.

In a way, it was poignant afternoon, since it was the last time she would be seen in public with the Prince before his departure two days later for a five-week tour of New Zealand, Australia, Venezuela and the USA. Like his previous tour, this could not be postponed at short notice following the engagement, since it had been arranged and prepared for months in advance. Similarly, because of the precision of those arrangements, there was no question of

including Lady Diana in the tour at all. If she had felt pangs of loneliness when, four months previously, the Prince had left for India, there was no doubt that she was utterly disconsolate at his departure now, bearing in mind that she had to endure her farewell to him in public, which made her misery all the greater. She bravely accompanied him to Heathrow Airport and to the foot of the aircraft steps, exchanged a brief embrace, and was escorted back to the VIP lounge from which even the blurred image of the telephoto camera lenses made clear the depth of her desolation as she lowered her head in tears.

Even for a level-headed young lady such as her, it must have seemed like the end of the world. But again, it was part of the necessary process of becoming accustomed, in her case with almost cruel speed, to the personal consequences of the official royal requirements. She

had the incalculable consolation of living, as she had since her engagement was announced, at Clarence House, where Queen Elizabeth the Queen Mother, herself a stranger almost sixty years earlier to the rigorous new demands of royal life, was able to give her the protection, encouragement and understanding necessary to keep her spirits up until her fiancé's return. During that long period, Lady Diana neither undertook nor took any part in official functions, but busied herself instead with the wealth of private business remorselessly looming up in connection with her forthcoming wedding.

Dropping in on the neighbours. Only a few miles from Highgrove, *overleaf,* Tetbury savoured its first visit by the Prince and Lady Diana on 22nd May when they attended a thanksgiving service and toured the General Hospital.

Meanwhile, newly arrived in the Antipodes with the Knighthood of the Order of Australia bestowed upon him by the Queen some days previously, Prince Charles was just as busy receiving from his hosts on the other side of the world tributes which left him in no doubt of the popularity of his decision to marry and the choice of a wife. He was constantly apologising for not having brought Lady Diana with him, and promising that he would do so "as soon as the whole thing was made legal." On his first full day in New Zealand there were tremendous cheers every time he mentioned Lady Diana, and again when he was congratulated officially on his engagement by the Prime Minister, Robert Muldoon. In Auckland, the Prince received a less obvious tribute in the form of a huge symbolic ball, chain and leg-iron ensemble: this had been fashioned in a New Zealand Royal Naval workshop and was presented by Jim Dolan "on behalf of all the depressed married men in New Zealand, and as a token to remind you of your folly in the years to come." At Lake Taupo, a Maori chief hinted that "this would be an ideal place for a Royal honeymoon," a remark which brought thunderous applause from the approving tribespeople. But the Prince said he couldn't oblige: plans were already afoot for a honeymoon on the Royal Yacht. Late in April, he saw a hairdressing demonstration at Hobart Technical College, and this gave him the opportunity to warm to his audience by bringing Lady Diana into the conversation. "I daresay," he said, "they are furiously practising Lady Diana haircuts somewhere in the background," and added that he would do well to learn some of the techniques "to save my fiancée from having to take a hairdresser with her when she goes on tours like this."

But it was not all fun. Quite apart from the daily round of official duties, which are always more onerous abroad than at home because of the comparative shortage of time available, Prince Charles was subjected to a few organised stunts in which the local Press appear to have been far from blameless. They bore on his forthcoming marriage, and on the whole he thought them in bad taste. At Long Hutt, near Wellington, very early on in the tour, he came unexpectedly face to face with half-a-dozen

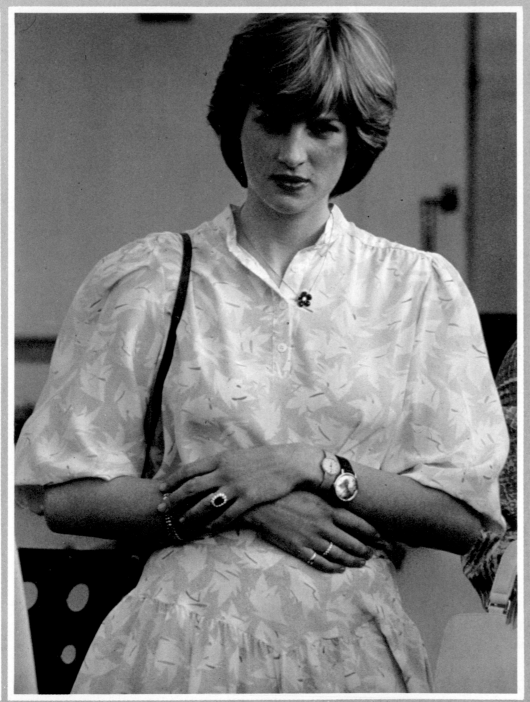

girls all identically made up and wearing hair-styles not greatly different from Lady Diana's. Prince Charles' displeasure was not assuaged by the presentation to him of half-a-dozen red roses, nor by half-a-dozen assurances that they only wanted "to make him feel at home." He dismissed it as "a put-up job" and moved on. At Bondi Beach, he almost fell victim to another, much older, stunt, when a well-proportioned and scantily-clad model, Brie Summers, attempted to approach him while he was taking one of his habitual early-morning dips in the sea off Bondi Beach. His detective was quick to spot her and raised the alarm, allowing the Prince sufficient headway to sprint angrily for his car.

Although these and similar ephemeral incidents are often cited as mere example of the

Above and left, **Lady Diana only just enjoys watching Prince** Charles play polo at Windsor in June, seeming preoccupied with possible danger associated with her own fall from a horse when she was ten. *Opposite,* breezy fashion at St Margaret's Westminster as Lady Diana, with Princess Margaret, Queen Elizabeth the Queen Mother and Prince Charles, watches the departure of Nicholas Soames and his bride Catherine Weatherall after their wedding. Another member of the Soames family, Clementine Hambro, was to be bridesmaid to Lady Diana that July.

occasional risks run by royalty, another much more sinister happening could not be dismissed so casually. Its occurrence became public during the weekend immediately following the Prince's return from the United States in early May, while he and Lady Diana celebrated their much longed-for reunion with a five-day holiday at Craigowan Lodge, back at Balmoral. News came through that secret illicit tapes had been made during the tour of some of Prince Charles' telephone conversations home, and that they contained personal and intimate exchanges between him and Lady Diana as well as more politically damaging references to Malcolm Fraser, the Australian Prime Minister and the Prince's official host during part of his tour. An English journalist and writer, Simon Regan, had apparently acquired transcripts of the tapes, the rights in which he was in the process of selling to a German weekly magazine. The affair sparked off endless controversy and caused a great burst of activity between the Palace and its lawyers who ultimately succeeded in serving an injunction against the magazine. Unfortunately, it came too late to be effective and the transcripts—innocuous, inaccurate and later proved totally spurious—were published. It was a sordid little affair which cannot have helped Lady Diana to come to terms easily with the potential pitfalls in the existence for which she was now being prepared.

The months of May, June and July were replete with a programme of the most varied activity for Lady Diana. Still of course unable to undertake any solo functions on behalf of the Queen, she was gradually introduced to many different facets of royal life from the inside whereas before, her experience of them, such as it was, was that of an onlooker only. Her mentor throughout this period was the Prince of Wales himself who, since only four days out of these three months were to be spent abroad, two in Paris and two in New York, could now devote himself entirely to promoting her apprenticeship at home. On May 9th they visited Broadlands, the Hampshire home of the late Lord Mountbatten, where Prince Charles opened an expansive and fascinating exhibition of Mountbatten memorabilia. As a memento of the visit, the couple planted trees in the grounds of the house, following a custom on which its

former owner had always insisted. Onlookers were thrilled by Lady Diana's lively participation in the fun of the occasion as, before a battery of cameras she exchanged witticisms with the Prince to the evident amusement of their hosts, Lord and Lady Romsey. Later she conducted her own little walkabout, meeting and talking to some of the hundreds who had come especially to see her, and all with an ease and naturalness rarely perceived in members of the Royal Family on duty. She was in her element with adults and children alike, and went so far as to pull one little boy's cap over his eyes, and to cradly a young mother's baby in her arms. These further indications of the alternative royal approach to come delighted all, may have perplexed a few, but saddened none.

Occasions of pomp and ceremony come thick and fast in May and June, and Lady Diana was introduced to them accordingly. Five days after the Broadlands trip she was present at Windsor Castle when the Queen entertained the President of Ghana to lunch and later, escorted by the Prince of Wales, presented new colours to the 1st Battalion of the Welsh Guards in a colourful ceremony in the Castle grounds. At the beginning of June Lady Diana accompanied the Prince to the Guards' Regimental Ball in the City of London, and was given first hand experience of the importance of his naval connections when she attended the annual church service and luncheon of Trinity House, of which the Prince is an Elder Brother and the Duke of Edinburgh is Master. Another taste of State occasion followed later that month when King Khalid of Saudi-Arabia paid a State Visit to Britain. This time Lady Diana attended not only the Queen's banquet at Buckingham Palace but also the King's return banquet at Claridge's, where her simple, pale blue-grey evening dress won plaudits from the hundreds who lined the street to see her arrive and leave. More pageantry followed when, on the Queen's official birthday on June 13th, Lady Diana watched the Trooping of the Colour ceremony. This may not have been the first occasion at which she was present at the ceremony, but it was the first time she had ever watched from the privileged position of the balconied window directly above the point where the Queen, with the Duke of Edinburgh,

Lady Diana's début — and what a first night! The occasion was a music recital, the venue Goldsmiths Hall in London, the date 9th March and the guest of honour, along with Prince Charles and his fiancée, was Princess Grace of Monaco. The dress was by Emanuels of London and will probably be remembered long after the other details of the evening have been forgotten. *Opposite page*, Princess Grace, herself a commoner before her marriage to Prince Rainier III of Monaco twenty five years earlier, compares notes with Lady Diana as they chat together at the reception prior to the recital. Already the future Princess of Wales seems entirely at ease, taking the inevitable public interest confidently in her stride.

the Prince of Wales and the Duke of Kent, Colonels of the Grenadier, Welsh and Scots Guards respectively, were positioned.

For this occasion, Lady Diana had arrived, shortly before the Queen rode onto Horse Guards Parade, in an open landau and in the company of Prince Andrew, receiving warm and prolonged applause from the usual capacity crowd of spectators as the carriage made its leisurely progrss across the well-known parade ground. What she could not have known until after the ceremony was over was that the Queen had been shot at as she rode into the approach road which links the Mall and Horse Guards. Reacting frenetically to the six revolver shots which rang out from within the crowd, the Queen's mare, Burmese, started, and made as if to bolt, but the Queen's horse-manship was more than sufficient to bring her in check. The Queen, though deathly white after the incident, soon regained her com-posure as scores of police dashed across the road to arrest the assailant, who was eventually charged under the 1842 Treason Act and given a five year sentence of imprisonment. News of the incident was received with particular alarm, coming as it did in the wake of the attempted assassinations of President Reagan and Pope John Paul II earlier in 1981. It was exceedingly unwelcome for Prince Charles and Lady Diana, for whose wedding security arrange-ments would now have to be tightened con-siderably. At the same time, it said a great deal for the spirit in which the Royal Family carries out its duties that there was no cancellation of the balcony appearance, at which the tra-ditional RAF flypast is witnessed after the ceremony, and that furthermore there was no sign on the faces of the Queen and her family of the acute apprehension they must have felt as they stood there, watching and waving. This unpleasant incident apart, the occasion brought Lady Diana the benefit of her first opportunity to experience the peculiar sensation of being up there on the balcony looking down instead of one of the many down on the ground looking up, and was no doubt intended to prepare her for the great day, barely six weeks distant, when she would appear there very much in her own right.

Opposite page and left, the dazzling arrival at Goldsmiths Hall that set the crowds buzzing and the cameras flashing: Lady Diana smiles gamely through it all. *Above*, the departure for Buckingham Palace.

For her next "first" Lady Diana was back at Windsor to attend the annual Garter ceremony at which the Queen, Prince Philip, Prince Charles and the Queen Mother were all present, and this was followed by the unique experience of the four days of Royal Ascot, where fashion experts and commentators put her under strict and constant scrutiny for signs of any independent line she might adopt in her choice of clothes for this prestigious social event. They were probably disappointed: on each day she wore pleasant but unspectacular outfits, steering a careful course between staidness and some of the more outrageous creations habitually sported by those seeking their own place in the annals of the ridiculous.

Lady Diana continued to accompany Prince Charles to several other functions until the early part of July when the preparations for their wedding were approaching the final

stages. It could fairly be claimed that by then she had been offered as much precognisance of her future responsibilities as it was possible to afford her in the short time available. For her part she seemed to have assimilated it all remarkably well: if she looked a little uneasy at some of the more formal occasions, it was only natural in one who could not be expected always to remember what was coming next. In more relaxed circumstances she was always very much *au fait* with what was expected of her, and she strove to supply it unprompted and with sincerity.

case of poor weather. He was additionally responsible for liaising with the police and the Armed Forces in connection with the position-ing of some three thousand police and as many troops up and down the entire processional route and in the precincts of both the Cathedral and the Palace. The timing of each event in the day's proceedings, from the opening of the Cathedral at 9 am to the arrival and departure of the principal guests, the processions to St Paul's and the ultimate homecomings, the facilit-ies for the Press and broadcasting media, with their hundred television cameras along the length of the route and inside the Cathedral, the seating arrangement in St Paul's itself, the flowers, the ushers, the domestic arrangements at Buckingham Palace—all had to be, and was, coordinated down to the last minute and square foot. Lord Maclean's job was from the start

Throughout the whole of her crash course in the art and science of being royal, arrange-ments for her wedding to the Prince had been proceeding at a furious, if ordered, pace. The man in charge of the entire organisation was the Lord Chamberlain, Lord Maclean, who executed his duties throughout with meticulous precision and the fullest attention to detail. The complete programme of processions and the

order of the service at St Paul's Cathedral was ready a month before the great day, a testimony to the speed and efficiency of the operation.

Eleven carriages from the stock of ceremonial vehicles in the Royal Mews had to be got ready, together of course with the horses to draw them and the teams of coachmen to drive them. Lord Maclean decided to play safe and set three more carriages—closed ones—aside in

made more difficult by the surprise choice of St Paul's Cathedral as the venue for the wedding, when it had been widely expected—indeed taken for granted in many quarters—that Westminister Abbey would as usual be chosen for the occasion. The change meant that many of the established precedents normally available to the organiser of royal weddings were of little immediate use, owing to the different layouts of the two churches and the varying lengths and routes of the processions. But it was generally agreed that the choice of St Paul's was a happy one: this mother church of

These pages and overleaf, comings and goings at Royal Ascot in mid-June. Lady Diana with a variety of escorts including Prince Charles and Princess Alexandra, maintains a comparatively low fashion profile at an event where hats count almost as much as horses.

the Commonwealth has been the theatre of many grand royal occasions of one kind or another for some fourteen centuries, and is moreover the largest Church of England building in the country. Prince Charles has worshipped there frequently and its record as the home of many major royal celebrations—Queen Victoria, King George V and Queen Elizabeth II held their Jubilee thanksgiving services there—made it an appropriate choice. A practical one too, since the Cathedral's impressive physical and architectural attributes include its lofty, light-giving nave, its resonant dome and

Wedding day at last. Serious faces, *opposite page,* **on** emerging from Buckingham Palace give way to smiles and waves from the bridegroom, his brother Prince Andrew, and the Queen and Prince Philip. And behind the veil the look of happiness from the bride in the Glass Coach.

galleries making it well suited to the performance of grandiose ceremonial music, and its massive seating capacity, some 20% greater than that of Westminster Abbey.

The competence which characterised Lord Maclean's punctilious arrangements was evidenced by the fact that even in the last full week before the wedding the betrothed couple, and Prince Charles in particular, did not have to

reduce the number or frequency of their official duties. On 20th and 21st July the Prince was on one of his perennial tours of his estates in the Duchy of Cornwall. He was back on the 22nd to join Lady Diana for a meeting at St Paul's for one of many wedding rehearsals necessary before the totally smooth running of the service could be properly assured. In the evening of that day he enjoyed the first of his wedding presents—a stag night at White's Club, of which he is a member, all expenses met by the Club. While the idea of holding a stag night a

Stages of a Royal Wedding. The billowing train on the Cathedral steps *(2)*, the first paces up the nave *(5)*, the vows *(1)*, the beautifully prepared Register with its signatures of eminent witnesses *(6)*, the progress towards the West Door *(3 and overleaf)* and the official portrait *(4)*.

1

2

3

full week before the wedding might seem an unusual one, it had the advantage of resolving any possible problems of hangovers on the wedding morning! But there need have been no worries—on the following day Prince Charles was up and about preparing himself for a garden party, at which Lady Diana was present, held by the Queen in the garden of Buckingham Palace to mark the International Year of Disabled People—a cause which the Prince has espoused throughout 1981.

5

4

The weekend before the wedding brought a pleasant mixture of public and private engagements for both the Prince and Lady Diana. On the 24th July, both went to Tidworth to visit the 1st Battalion of the 22nd (Cheshire) Regiment who were stationed there, and they stayed at Tidworth for the following day's polo match in which Prince Charles played for the Navy against the Army. It was a typical gesture of an active man whose appetite for sport has always remained strong that only four days before his wedding, with all its national and international

6

implications, he should consent to risk his neck at this very physical and competitive game. Some considered it foolhardy, too, in the light of complete disarray into which any serious injury to the Prince could throw the long-planned wedding arrangements. However, in deference to the memory of his previous falls from horses, both on and off the polo field, he continued to use the face mask he had adopted some months earlier, and had a whole fleet of doctors, ambulances and, thoughtfully, veterinary teams standing by for the worst. These precautions did little to allay Lady Diana's fears and throughout

the game she sat nervously biting lips and knuckles as she watched her future husband throw himself into some very brave tackles. The following day, a Sunday, saw him playing polo yet again — his last appearance on the field as a bachelor — as he played for England's second team against Spain at Windsor Great Park.

With many members of the Royal Family present plus some of the guests for the wedding, including Mrs Nancy Reagan with her posse of security men, the Press were out in force and on the whole they gave, understandably enough, more attention to Lady Diana than to the progress of the match itself. Wherever she walked she was pursued and anticipated by an army of photographers anxious to obtain the last pictures of her as a single girl, and in spite of the best efforts of a hopelessly overstretched contingent of police and officials it soon became impossible for her to go anywhere without her unwanted escort of jostling pressmen and the incessant whirring and clicking of a hundred cameras. Her concern for the safety of Prince Charles was an additional strain on her and halfway through the match this hitherto calm and patient model of self-assurance broke down, fleeing the field in tears under the comforting arm of Lady Romsey. Lady Diana had come a long way since her engagement, but at that point the words of her fiancé when he first pointed out the disadvantages of his life-style must have assumed a graphic and terrible relevance.

It was with some relief that the Prince was able to assure everyone the following day that Lady Diana had quickly recovered from the emotional strain of the occasion which, apart from the swift private attendances at St Paul's for the last-minute touches, was the last on which the British public would be able to see the girl who would soon become its next Princess of Wales. By that Monday morning the streets of London were tight with traffic as visitors suddenly poured into the capital to take up their places mainly, at this stage, near St Paul's. It was a full two days before the wedding, but out came the camping equipment, the stoves, picnic hampers, blankets, quilts and shopping bags, and from then on the pavements from the Cathedral to the Palace gradually became more thickly lined with a population eager to witness and take part in probably the most magnificent celebrations of their lifetime.

Officially the public celebrations began on the night prior to the wedding when, in the

The solemnity of the Archbishop of Canterbury's final blessing *(4)* is shared by the Royal Family. Then the bride, groom and congregation sit *(2)* for the lesson read by Mr George Thomas. After the signing of the Registers the Prince and Princess begin their long walk *(3)* from the Dean's Aisle to the West Door *(1)* of the Cathedral. The following pages encapsulate the universal joy of the royal couple's appearance on the Cathedral steps and the bridal and family processions back to Buckingham Palace.

3

4

A prolonged curtain call for the Prince and Princess on the Palace balcony—at first alone, then joined by bridesmaids, pages and eventually family guests, *overleaf*. Their smiles say it all as they respond first to the crowd's mighty acclaim and ultimately to its demands for a public show of affection.

balmiest evening weather and almost as a proclamation of intent as to the scale and sparkle of the following day's proceedings, a mighty display of fireworks was staged at Hyde Park. Promoted as comparable in size and spectacle only to the great Royal Fireworks of 1749 for which Handel wrote his suite of music of that title, the event drew, as it was designed to, something in the order of half a million people from all sides of London—or, if truth be

told, from all parts of the world. For Londoners particularly, with their families young and old, it was a dazzling free show of a lifetime which brought them flocking to this most famous of all London parks. The Royal Family was there in strength of course, together with 150 distinguished guests, the majority of whom were members of reigning or exiled European royal families and mostly distant relatives of the House of Windsor. One notable absentee was the lady of the moment, the celebrated bride-to-be, who had made the forgivable decision not to face the cameras again, and to have an early night—her last at Clarence House—in readiness for the greatest day of her life.

The principal attraction in terms of person-

Above, **a study in navy and white as Commander Prince** Charles, Midshipman Prince Andrew, the pages in cadet uniform and Prince Edward join the bride and her five bridesmaids, all in ivory silk, for Patrick Lichfield's official photograph in the Throne Room of Buckingham Palace. *Opposite,* family friends become relations as parents, grandparents, brothers, sisters and cousins swell the group. The Queen and Queen Mother are there; Viscount Linley stands between Prince Andrew and Prince Philip, while behind Mrs Shand Kydd and Lord Spencer are Ruth Lady Fermoy, Viscount Althorp, and Lady Jane and Mr Robert Fellowes.

alities at least was the Prince of Wales himself, who began the business of the evening by lighting the first of 101 beacons which would carry the inaugural message to all corners of the British Isles: the chain stretched as far south as the Channel Islands and as far north as the Shetlands, and from Northern Ireland, Land's End and Caernarvon in the west to East

Left, Patrick Lichfield's classic photograph of the royal couple. *Above,* the bride alone; a warm blush in a mist of tulle and lace. *Opposite,* for comparison, one of Lord Snowdon's earlier portraits. *Overleaf,* the start of a royal honeymoon.

Anglia and the Isle of Thanet in the east. This, the bridegroom's symbolic act, recalled to most who witnessed it, the June evening when his mother had ignited the first of a similar number of fires in Windsor Great Park to herald the Silver Jubilee thanksgiving in 1977. For that celebration, the lighting of beacons and the firework display took place on two different occasions: now the two were merged into the single event and the effect was truly spectacular.

The distinguished guests and just a few thousand people who arrived in good enough time to select their vantage points at leisure secured the full benefit of this triumphal display which was in concept an experience for the ear as well as for the eye. They had the

JUST MARRIED

good fortune, unhappily denied to hundreds of thousands of others, to see the focal point of the event—a mock palace façade, ringed with artillery, against which the fireworks were set off—and to hear the thrilling and appropriate blend of music and explosive as the attendant massed bands and choirs burst into symphony and song. Although this aesthetic impact of the occasion was lost on the majority of comers, some of whom were still crowding through the Park gates even as the programme ended, all

The President of the United States of America and Mrs Reagan

Opulence and simplicity at St James's Palace as priceless jewellery, plate, glassware and china are set cheek by jowl with teacosies and pincushions, *overleaf.* The two month exhibition of wedding presents included the bride's wedding dress.

who did attend saw and marvelled at the successive sallies of soaring rocketry as it rose skyward and spread high and wide into the warm and festive night air, with explosions which shook the very ground for hundreds of yards around. The *pièce de résistance* was a giant Catherine Wheel, a mechanically operated device some forty feet across, which produced and spread flame over a diameter of over a hundred feet. With this, as with almost every other item in the programme, the gasps and hoots of delight were total and genuine; the applause notwithstanding the absence of a visible recipient, was spontaneous and appreciative.

If, following the spectacle of that evening, and on the verge of one of the most momentous days in the history of the Royal Family, the two principal participants managed to get any sleep, it was a short lived luxury. Over at Clarence House, Lady Diana was up at 6 am to begin long and meticulous preparations, and like some princess from mediaeval days about to embark upon a marriage of state, was surrounded by attendants and those excelling in their art busily working around her to produce perfection of fashion and beauty. Among them was her hairdresser Kevin Shanley, whose job it

was to retain in the styling the basic simplicity and lightness of her coiffure whilst adapting it sufficiently to suit the addition of a tiara. Lady Diana's tiara was an ornate but unobtrusive diamond creation from the Spencer family heirlooms, incorporating an intricate entwined star and flower design with a heart-shaped centrepiece: apart from a pair of heavy earrings, it was the only jewellery she chose to wear. Her make-up for the day was the responsibility of

daybreak and beginning to make themselves heard even through its solid walls, there would have been little prospect of any normal night's sleep. As it was, with his acute sense of history and occasion, he spent time listening at his bedroom window, drinking in those unique sounds of expectant crowds waiting to cheer their future sovereign to his wedding. Never reluctant to confess his emotion at spontaneous and sincere demonstrations of loyalty and love for

Barbara Daly who had set up her box in Lady Diana's dressing room the previous day. She admitted the delicate nature of her job: the bride's fair and fresh complexion made it unnecessary to go in for heavy coverage. "Lady Diana blushes very prettily," she said, adding that she would attempt to keep her applications to a minimum in order to let those blushes radiate through.

For Prince Charles too it was a morning of early and intense preparation. With the crowds outside Buckingham Palace astir well before

The Prince and his bride receive a loyal welcome and farewell as they drive through Gibraltar toward the harbour where the Royal Yacht Britannia, *overleaf,* awaits to take them on their two-week cruise in the Mediterranean.

his family and the Crown, from whatever quarter they may come, the Prince told the Lord Mayor of London at the Guildhall the following November how he heard and marked well the surging noise below so that "I could one day tell my children exactly what it was like."

By no stretch of the imagination could this

colourful celebration be said to be taking place in the happiest of national or international circumstances. The world was in economic recession, tortured by the perennial antipathy between East and West and by troubles in Afghanistan, Poland and the Middle East; and a deep concern about the threat of nuclear weapons encompassed us all. At home the insoluble Northern Ireland problem, with its wholesale waste of lives and property, continued. A decreasing standard of living matched a rising rate of unemployment, and frustrations which certainly owed something to these deteriorating social and economic conditions found

Almost alone at last, the Prince and Princess wave goodbye to the Rock as Britannia glides away. There were few sightings until the Yacht reached Egypt, *overleaf,* where President and Mrs Sadat received them for a short visit. It was just seven weeks before Sadat's assassination.

terrifying and unprecedented expression in enormous street riots in Brixton, Toxteth and the disadvantaged suburbs of a dozen major British cities. It is often said that the heavier the stress, the better the British are at forgetting it even for a short time when a convenient opportunity arises. Much to the disgust of commentators in Soviet and some Eastern Euro-

66

A week after their return to Balmoral, the Brig o' Dee was the location for a long-awaited camera call when dozens of cameramen were able to take pictures of a relaxed, suntanned couple at the peak of contentment. Jokes and pithy remarks flew from the Prince and Princess to the photographers, and a bouquet of flowers found their way back in return. The result was a profusion of excellent photographs and the restoration of the good relationships between the Press and Palace which had been so seriously endangered at the beginning of the year.

pean newspapers, who were quick to point out the unpalatable comparison between the glamour of the wedding and the daunting reality of everyday life lurking in the background, the promise was of a day of unbridled celebration, come what may. And true to form, as the events of the day unfolded, effortlessly and with inexorable precision, the general feeling radiating throughout the crowded streets and in the homes of millions who watched and listened

was one of confidence and renewal in an environment soured by malice and despair.

By nine o'clock that morning the sun was well up, the sky was blue with only a modest patchwork of cloud, and the air was warm. Crowds estimated at over a million had long since foresaken makeshift breakfast arrangements and had secured their positions round Cathedral and Palace alike and along the two miles of processional route that separated them. Independent Televison News com-

fusion of royal purple and blue—provided by some 6,000 plants. The flagstaffs in St James's Park were even more ornate: each was surrounded by three spiked poles draped with Union Jacks, and supported a platter of fresh yellow, white and cream flowers which looked almost ready to spill over onto the salvia-and geranium-bedded lawns below. Beyond Admiralty Arch, Trafalgar Square and the Strand displayed a more modest array of red, white and blue banners linked with bunting, and

missioned an airship, afloat over London, which recorded unique pictures of the pattern of shifting colour as the multitude surged, eleven military bands marched to their appointed places, and three thousand police and as many troops took up position in front of some eight thousand crush barriers. Down on the ground the views were just as breathtaking: the red carpet was already laid (though at this stage covered by a protective sheet of thick polythene) down the steps of St Paul's; the balcony of Buckingham Palace sported its famous crimson drapes—an indication that the tradition of balcony appearances, never promised but always expected, would be maintained to delight the crowds after the wedding ceremony. Lining the Mall were 150 gold-crowned and tasselled flagstaffs, each bearing an enormous Union Flag, which at a distance seemed almost to peep from the lush deep green of that well-established avenue of trees in summer leaf. Each of the intervening lamp-posts was decorated with a basket of delicate summer flowers—verbenias, petunias, phlox—a pro-

backed by some really extravagant montages which for some weeks before had been going up on the premises of commercial firms and administrative offices lining the route.

It was against this background that the first of the two-and-a-half thousand guests had begun to make their way to St Paul's Cathedral. Many were personal friends of the bride and groom and their families: perhaps the most celebrated of all were Lady Diana's three flatmates, Carolyn Pride, Virginia Pitman and Anne Bolton, who over the last six months had found themselves catapulted into public recognition. Then there were racing acquaintances of Prince Charles—Nick Gaselee, the trainer of his

63

National Hunt horses and the father of one of the bridesmaids, and Mark Floyd and Richard Linley, two of his jockeys. Other friends included Susan George the actress; Harry Secombe and Spike Milligan, former exponents of the art of Goonery; former girlfriends like Lady Jane Wellesley and Sabrina Guinness; his former headmaster at Cheam, Mr Peter Beck; Lord Butler, Master of Trinity College during Prince Charles' time there between 1967 and 1970; and Lord Soames, a family friend and grandfather of another bridesmaid, Clementine Hambro. In addition, staff from Highgrove, the couple's future home in Gloucestershire, were invited, as were staff who had long since retired or left service, including a middle-aged couple from Eleuthera who had kept house for the Prince when he was once a guest of Countess Mountbatten there. Alongside personal friends came representatives of foreign and Commonwealth countries some of whom, like Mrs Ghandi of India and Mr Fraser of

Australia, were also personally known to Prince Charles if not to his fiancée. Then came the vast contingent of royal cousins—the ex-Kings Constantine of Greece, Michael of Roumania, Simeon of Bulgaria and Crown Prince Alexander of Yugoslavia—all, like Prince Charles himself, directly descended from or closely related to Queen Victoria. Members of royal families outside Europe included the Crown Princes of Jordan, Japan and Siam and the Kings of Nepal, Samoa, Malaya and Tonga—the latter, King Tafa 'ahau Tupou IV of Tonga, 28 stone of Pacific Island authority, brought his own equally im-

pressive carved chair which would accommodate his large form more adequately than anything St Paul's Cathedral had to offer.

At just after ten o'clock, minor members of the Royal Family—the Beauforts, the Abel-Smiths, the Fifes and the Southesks—left Buckingham Palace by car, and ten minutes later a line of black, shining limousines bore the nineteen members of reigning European royalties in order of rank (i.e. kings before grand dukes

and grand dukes before reigning princes) and then in order of length of reign. So the procession was headed by King Baudouin of the Belgians and Queen Fabiola, followed by the affable King Olav V of Norway with his son and daughter-in-law Crown Prince Harald and Crown Princess Sonja. Queen Margarethe II of Denmark came next, with her husband Prince Henrik; then King Carl XVI of Sweden and Queen Silvia. Following them came Queen Beatrix of the Netherlands with Prince Claus; Grand Duke Jean and Grand Duchess Josephine-Charlotte of Luxemburg, Prince Franz-Josef II and Princess Gina of Liechtenstein, and Princess Grace of Monaco accompanied by her son

A touch of Rob Roy at the Braemar Games. The Princess of Wales was the new girl at the Highland Games at Braemar in early September, and she came appropriately dressed in plaid and a Tam o' Shanter, and bearing a spray of Scots heather, *opposite right.* Lady Sarah Armstrong-Jones, Princess Margaret's seventeen-year-old daughter, and the

Princess of Wales' chief bridesmaid, was also there, *opposite left,* with her brother Viscount Linley. As always it was a happy occasion as well, it seems, as instructive for the Princess who was kept abreast of events by Prince Charles— all part of her long term introduction to the major occasions which form the annual pattern of the Royal Family's personal life and public duties.

69

Prince Albert, who deputised for his father Prince Rainier. It was about the largest gathering of crowned heads and their representatives in Britain since at least the Coronation in 1953, and however much of a family occasion this was intended to be, the rank and position of the guests made it impossible not to regard it as a ceremony of State.

Meanwhile, cars containing the five bridesmaids and the two pages, all headed by Lady Sarah Armstrong-Jones, slipped quietly away from Clarence House and took them to the Cathedral. Lady Sarah looked suddenly very grown up with her long hair and confident features, as she gathered her little brood of younger bridesmaids round her.

Shortly after 10.20, the Queen's carriage procession at last left Buckingham Palace. For the tens of thousands lining the roadway round the Queen Victoria Memorial and for the formidable array of British and foreign press and television cameramen who had set up their equipment there, this was the signal for the real start of the day's business. As the military band inside the Palace forecourt played the National Anthem for the first time, out of the precincts came a couple of divisions of the Sovereign's Escort followed by the first carriage —a shining open semi-State postillion landau drawn by four splendid Oldenburg Grey horses. Inside, the Queen, in an aquamarine coat of loose-pleated crêpe-de-chine, looked somewhat grave, mildly curious at the cheering crowds, while at her side the Duke of Edinburgh, wearing the uniform of an Admiral of the Fleet, the Order of the Garter and a long row of medals winking and jingling as the journey continued, chatted purposefully to her and flashed the occasional beaming smile at the crowd.

Behind them in an open State landau came Queen Elizabeth the Queen Mother, thankfully recovered from the slight illness caused by an ulcer following a fall at Ascot in June, and already allowing her customary radiance to appear as if this were very much *her* day. On the verge of her eighty-first birthday, and dressed in almond green with the osprey plumes of her powder-puff hat trembling in the slight breeze, she looked as happy as ever, and the crowds, high on the royal rejoicing, applauded her for it. Beside her sat her youngest grandson, Prince

Edward, 17 years old and nattily dressed in topper and tails, bearing himself with the modesty becoming a young man honoured with the task of escorting one of the best loved of all members of the Royal Family. Following another division of the Sovereign's Escort came the two Princesses—Anne with her splashy sunflower hat perched precariously forward over her temple, and Margaret, more conventionally in a warm, azalea-peach creation. With them rode a smiling Captain Mark Phillips in uniform, and Viscount Linley, at 20 the natural escort for his mother, looking serious in morning dress but very much the part.

Then came those members of the Royal Family representing King George V's younger

sons: first the Gloucesters—the ladies in periwinkle and hyacinth, with the Duchess looking serene and responsive to the welcoming spectators; and Princess Alice observing with interest everything going on round her: the Duke, uniformed, smiling indulgently as his impish son the Earl of Ulster fidgeted and climbed about in his seat. Then came the solemn figure of the Duke of Kent, imposing in scarlet uniform and bearskin, with his popular and accomplished wife and his adolescent children the Earl of St Andrews and Lady Helen Windsor. In the sixth carriage came those unknown quantities of the family, Prince and Princess Michael of Kent— Prince Michael in his red-capped uniform of Major in the Royal Fusiliers waved stolidly as

his tall elegant wife watched approvingly in her cool white dress and floppy, wide-brimmed hat. Last of all came the Ogilvys—both Princess Alexandra and her husband good-humoured and spontaneous while their children James and Marina savoured the excitement of the charged atmosphere.

For now came the time of the man of the moment. At precisely 10.30 a division of the Prince of Wales' Escort emerged from the inner courtyard of Buckingham Palace followed by the beautiful 1902 State Postillion Landau carrying the Prince himself. Wearing the uniform of a Commander of the Royal Navy, with the Order of the Garter and his Coronation and Silver Jubilee medals, he seemed at first rather nonplussed by the deafening cheers, the frantically waving flags and the placards of welcome and good wishes. But as the low-slung carriage

bowled round the Queen Victoria Memorial, hauled by four Greys with their special silver mane-dressings, he spent what seemed like ages in earnest conversation with Prince Andrew, his chief supporter in midshipman uniform, then requited the rapture of his admirers by breaking out into an appreciative smile and a modest acknowledgement of his tumultuous reception.

Shortly after that the exquisite Glass Coach, now seventy years old, made its first jolting movements from the yard of Clarence House into the approach road to the Mall. It bore the jewel of the occasion, Lady Diana, on her journey of high destiny, scarely visible behind a

The Princess of Wales became the queen of Welsh hearts from the minute she set foot in the North of Wales on 27th October. With Prince Charles she attended Deeside Leisure Centre and heard the best of Welsh choral singing at first hand, *overleaf.*

froth of tulle which seemed to be bundled into the closed carriage, blocking out all but her veiled face and the proud, broad features of her father Earl Spencer. The Glass Coach was only five minutes behind the carriage containing the Prince of Wales, and both parties were now irretrievably on their way to the country's grandest altar.

The Prince of Wales and Prince Andrew arrived at the Cathedral shortly before 11 o'clock. They strode purposefully up its steps, cheered

on by the crowd, to where the clergy waited to greet them at the great West Door. Among them was the Archibishop of Canterbury, who would conduct the marriage, swathed in resplendent silver-grey robes with gold thread-worked design—both cope and mitre worn for the first time of this day of days. To him Prince Charles had much to say as Prince Andrew checked twice that he had brought the ring. Then with the final good wishes from the Archbishop, Purcell's rousing March for the Prince of Denmark was struck up and the Prince, with his brothers on either side, strode, almost casually, up that famous aisle, nodding cheerfully left and right at recognised faces.

Outside, another tumult of cheers heralded the arrival of the bride as the Glass Coach drew up ready for her to emerge to full public view. It was at that moment that everyone could appreciate the full splendour of that dress, with

bride's throat was devoid of jewellery, in stark but winning contrast to the heavy romantic frill of taffeta and lace which topped the bodice. At the centre of the bodice was a huge Victorian bow which complemented the dated design of the bridemaids' dresses and harked back to the

Flowers and Welsh dolls for the Princess; advice and explanation for the Prince. The royal visitors study the extensive exhibitions of patriotic art and craft at Deeside in North Wales. *Overleaf*, Prince Charles returned to the scene of his Investiture as Prince of Wales twelve years earlier as he took his Princess to Caernarvon Castle. In cold, cheerless weather they sat in seats which the Queen and Prince Philip occupied at the ceremony within the ruined walls of the Castle which looks out across the Menai Strait towards Anglesey.

its voluminous gown and its boned and fitted bodice into which 10,000 pearls and mother-of-pearl sequins were sewn. At the sleeves and fronting the bodice were generous ornamentations of intricately embroidered antique lace, ruffed and panelled from a flounce of Carrickmacross lace once presented by Queen Mary to the Royal School of Needlework. The

style prevalent at the time of another Prince of Wales' wedding in the heady days of Victorian prosperity. Behind the bride, as she began to make her way up the Cathedral steps, her 25-foot long train unfolded and cascaded down like a stream in full surge behind her. Of the whole, the crowds had an all too fleeting vision, but they cheered every moment of her progress until she disappeared from view.

Inside the Cathedral she too was welcomed by the clergy who then formed the procession to lead her to her waiting bridegroom. The organ and orchestra exploded with the initial notes of the Trumpet Tune by Jeremiah Clarke, himself an organist at St Paul's in the early years of the eighteenth century. The bride, now on the arm of her father, looked as confident as could be wished, with her splendid waterfall bouquet of myrtle, freesia and gardenia, cuttings of stephanotis. orchid and odontoglossum

and a spray of those faintly golden Earl Mountbatten roses. Having, after a full three and a half minutes' progress over some 650 feet of red carpet, arrived at the dais where Prince Charles stood, Lady Diana, shimmering in the floodlights, paused by his side: they exchanged a word and each clutched the other's hand momentarily—a gesture which the Queen, with the smile of one who knows how it must be, was not to slow to notice.

At this point the service began with the hymn "Christ is made the sure Foundation," a dedicatory hymn with words admirably suited, by innuendo at least, to the marriage ceremony. It was gloriously arranged, and the uncanny silence at the end of it signified a temporary

These studies of the Prince and Princess of Wales during the closing stages of their first day in Wales show that they had lost none of their enthusiasm despite the heavy programme of this whistle-stop tour.

Overleaf, **a kiss for Lord** Snowdon at Caernarvon Castle. He had been created Constable of the Castle shortly before Prince Charles' Investiture and he now welcomed the royal couple on this Welsh visit. Elsewhere the Prince and Princess continued to meet the people and, *far right,* the Princess found time to exchange a brief word with her lady-in-waiting, Anne Beckwith-Smith.

end to the pageantry and the beginning of the serious business of the hour. The Dean of St Paul's came forward to introduce the service with those time-honoured words on the Christian meaning and purpose of marriage. No known impediments to the marriage were declared and the Archbishop then came forward to administer the vows. Here, Lady Diana allowed herself a momentary fluster as she repeated the names of Prince Charles in the wrong order—Philip Charles Arthur George—much to the Prince's amusement. Later, however, it was his turn to fluff his lines as he promised to share all *her* goods. But the Archbishop didn't make them go through it again till it was right, and was content eventually to pronounce them man and wife together. That pronouncement was met by a roar of applause from the crowd outside the Cathedral whose noisy reaction to each significant juncture in the service was clearly audible within the Cathedral walls. And this was of course the most telling moment of all, as Lady Diana, until recently a kindergarten schoolteacher, became Princess of Wales, Countess of Chester, Duchess of Cornwall, Duchess of Rothesay etc. etc. and the third lady in the land after the Queen and Queen Mother.

Appropriately the musical celebration started, with a vigorous, shrill and triumphant arrangement by the Welsh composer William Mathias of words from Psalm 67: "Let the people praise Thee O God...Let the nations rejoice and be glad...The earth shall bring forth her increase." Then came the lesson, not so much read as intoned by none other than Mr George Thomas, Speaker of the House of Commons and a great personal friend of Prince Charles: "Though I speak with the tongues of angels and have not love..."—the words rang out to an audience attentive as if it were hearing them for the first time.

Then followed the Archbishop of Canterbury's own thoughts on this most spectacular of occasions, thoughts which he introduced with a cliché that had been on everyone's lips since the engagement was announced. "This is the stuff of which fairy tales are made," he submitted, rather severly, and went on to put in its proper place the fairytale view that the marriage is the end of the story. He preferred the Christian view which "sees the wedding

Day two of the tour of Wales saw the Prince and Princess travelling down towards the south of the Principality, initially in dry but breezy weather which caught the Princess' ostrich-feathered hat, *opposite*. Then, after the service at St David's Cathedral, *below and overleaf*, the rain came down with a vengeance. It was no time to disregard umbrellas, but both the Prince and Princess found it quicker if less comfortable to ignore the weather. There were too many people to meet, and from them the couple collected so many sprays and bunches of flowers that the police escort had to be called in to deal with them all, *overleaf*.

day not as the place of arrival but the place where the adventure begins." He introduced the comparison of some Catholic marriages in which crowns are held over the heads of the couple to symbolise that they are kings and queens of creation. "All couples on their wedding day are royal couples," he continued. "Those who are married live happily ever after the wedding day if they persevere in the real adventure which is the royal task of creating each other and creating a more loving world." It was a broadly simple, yet structurally intricate address, with its interwoven allegories all coming together in timely and harmonious conclusion. The sanctity of the marriage was well stressed, as was the premise that "we as human beings can help to shape this world; we are not victims." He ended with more concrete realism in voicing the hope that "the burdens we lay upon the couple be matched by the love with which we support them in the years to come." Few would not have added "Amen" to that.

The choir then sang Parry's powerful anthem, beloved of four monarchs at their Coronations, "I was Glad," the words of which, taken from Psalm 122, incorporate the prayer "Peace be within thy walls and plenteousness within thy

Palaces." When it was over, the Prince of Wales and his Princess were kneeling at the High Altar, a stark, gold-ornamented fixture in Sicilian marble amid the rich browns, golds and reds on all sides, where, in the best tradition of English choral singing, the Lesser Litany was intoned and sung, and where in fulfilment of the ecumenical objectives Prince Charles had set, prayers were said by a former Archbishop of Canterbury, the Roman Catholic Archbishop of Westminster, the Moderator of the Church of Scotland and a member of the Anglican Community of the Resurrection. This latter was the first to mention by name and title "Diana, Princess of Wales," and of course it was the day on which she entered the Church of England liturgy in which morning and evening prayers are said for members of the Royal Family.

And it was very much her moment next. As the second hymn, she personally had chosen Cecil Spring Rice's poem of dedication and spiritual allegory, "I Vow to Thee, my Country," sung to Gustav Holst's serene and imposing music, and bringing with it the realisation that this was not just a marriage ceremony but also an occasion at which the bride in particular must dedicate herself to the service of her country.

The Archbishop then gave his final blessing and, as the sung "Amens" faded away the south transept erupted with a drumroll and fanfare heralding Sir David Willcocks' soaring arrangement of the National Anthem which would bring the service to a memorable conclusion. But the ceremonial was not yet over: after the National Anthem, the clergy moved from the sanctuary to the Dean's Aisle to the right: the bride and groom followed, with the immediate families of each bringing up the rear. The Dean's Aisle was the venue for the signing of the two Registers—a church register for the parish records, and a royal register. The signatories were, in addition to the Archbishop of Canterbury, the Prince—signing himself for the first time "Charles P", and the new Princess, signing for the last time "Diana Spencer": then the Queen and Prince Philip, the Queen Mother, Prince Andrew, Prince Edward, Princess Anne and Lady Sarah Armstrong-Jones. On the bride's side, her father Lord Spencer, her mother Mrs Shand Kydd, and her grandmother Ruth Lady Fermoy added their signatures. For the congre-

gation there was of course a hiatus, which was entertainingly filled by the performance of two pieces from Handel's Oratorio "Samson." The Aria "Let the Bright Seraphim" was given a virtuoso rendition, bright, angelic and trumpet-clear, by the New Zealand operatic singer Kiri Te Kanawa; then followed the brilliant Chorus "Let their Celestial Concerts All Unite," which the Bach Choir and Orchestra performed with ease and clarity, and a power which had everyone listening intently. It was the culmination in fitting vein of what Prince Charles himself had wanted, "a musical experience as well as an emotional one," alive with joyful sounds.

As this performance came to its close, the members of the two families resumed their places to await the final fanfare from the Whispering Gallery. It greeted the appearance of the Prince and Princess of Wales from the Dean's Aisle and the beginning of their first walk together as man and wife. The effect as they turned into the centre of the Quire and headed westward was visionary: the tall, slim, serious, occasion-conscious naval Commander linked arm in arm with his young and attractive wife, her veil now thrown back to reveal that famous blush and modest smile. They stopped to pay homage to the Queen, and then, to the music of Elgar's Pomp and Circumstance March No. 4, it was smiles all the way as they proceeded down the aisle to the West Door, the sunshine and the immensity of faces, flags and noise. For the first time, the crowds saw their new Princess of Wales emerge from the double colonnaded front of the Cathedral, and there was a pandemonium of cheers, shouts, bells, rattles, whistles and hooters, all to the evident delight of the Princess. She in turn, prompted by Prince Charles, waved victoriously back to another roar of approbation. Then they were on their way down the steps to the waiting landau as the Queen and the whole Royal Family clustered round the Cathedral door to watch their departure.

The journey back, of course, was an exercise in making friends without really trying. There

Under the watchful eye of her detective, the Princess of Wales passes by the crowds who lined the streets of every town and village, with a hand-shake or flowers at almost every step, *opposite.* Like the Prince, she became soaked; her hair and the feathers of her hat were bedraggled, *above right and overleaf.* Equally dampened in all but spirit, *overleaf,* the crowd's ubiquitous presence was a measure of the tour's success.

was not an unhappy face to be seen; just a sea of smiles and laughter, jubilation, goodwill and congratulation. As the landau sped down the Mall and took the final turn of the Queen Victoria Memorial, both its occupants had every right to be gratified by the response they elicited from their future subjects. A final thoughtful gesture remained to be exposed: in the forecourt of Buckingham Palace a hundred or so disabled people, specially invited by the Prince and Princess in this International Year of Disabled People, had been gathered together for the brief but privileged close-up glimpse of the couple as they passed into the inner courtyard of the Palace.

Behind the Prince and Princess came the fleet of carriages carrying the other members of the family, plus of course Lord Spencer, who rode

with the Queen and Mrs Shand Kydd, who was escorted by the Duke of Edinburgh. Behind that procession the jostling crowd began to surge earnestly up the Mall to witness the balcony appearances. They were not long in coming, and the cheer that went up as the couple stepped forward into full view defied all superlatives. The Prince and Princess were plainly delighted with this incontrovertible expression of loyalty and affection—the banners full of pithy phrases of greeting, the flags of all colours and sizes, beautifully made blue and silver balloons bearing their portraits and names bobbing and floating restlessly above the heads that strained for the better view. Then the raucous choruses of the National Anthem and "Rule Britannia" gave way to shouts for "Charles", "Di", "the Queen". . . . And eventually the Queen appeared —as on her journey back from the Cathedral, noticeably more happy and relaxed than at the beginning of the day. With her came not only the family but also the Spencers, enjoying a unique moment of public attention, and the bridesmaids and pages all spick and span, the younger ones delighting the crowds with their childish antics.

In all the bride and groom came back, with some or all of their families, four times and each time the crowd yelled for more. At one point Prince Charles was so caught up in the infectious spirit of the proceedings that he took his wife's hand and in a gallant, almost anachronistic gesture, kissed it. This drew whistles of approval from below but it was not enough for them. "Kiss her! Kiss her!" they shouted, and, to the astonishment of all he did. It was probably the first public kiss to be administered on that famous balcony, but no one could possibly have objected that it was in any way out of place.

As eventually, at the end of this giant curtain call, the doors of the Palace closed for the last time it seemed more evident than ever that, as the 19th century historian Bagehot said: "A princely marriage is the brilliant edition of a universal fact and as such rivets mankind. We have come to believe it is natural to have a virtuous sovereign, and that domestic virtues are as likely to be found on thrones as they are eminent when there." Despite the heavy wording the proceedings of this wedding morning bore witness to the fundamental truth: in a gloriously supple display of ceremonial hallmarked with the British genius for pageantry

and colour this was a day of pure romance in a palsied world, and act of personal dedication and public devotion both rare and utterly significant as part of the history of our ten centuries of monarchy. It was part of the living theatre of kingship, with which, thanks to the immediacy of its reporting by the graphic medium of television, all onlookers, whether subjects under the kingship or not, could adopt as a manifestation of their own personal identities and sense of commitment. As the Archbishop said: "All

couples on their wedding day are royal couples."

Three hours later the honeymoon began. Many countries had invited the Prince and Princess to spend it as their guests, and other suggestions and speculation as to a suitable venue (based mostly on previous royal honeymoons or on Prince Charles' known favourite haunts) came thick and fast from all sides. Details of the chosen tour were kept strictly secret until, within two weeks of the wedding day, it was almost grudgingly revealed that the

Royal Yacht Britannia would take the couple for a Mediterranean cruise: indeed it was this news, with the announcement that Gibraltar would be the starting point, which led the King and Queen of Spain to withdraw their acceptance of the wedding invitation. This, however, was as far as official disclosure went: in a firm and determined attempt to ensure the royal couple as much peace and privacy as possible, the Palace gave no futher advance details of ports of call except in the case of the visit to Egypt late in the journey.

It was however strongly suspected, in view of the sudden temporary closure of the Mountbatten exhibition at Broadlands, that part of the honeymoon would be spent there, and sure enough, shortly before the wedding day itself those suspicions were officially confirmed. In a way it was an obvious choice, and certainly most appropriate, prompted as it no doubt was by Prince Charles' close connections with the Mountbattens, and following tradition in that it was there that the Queen and Prince Philip went to spend the first part of their honeymoon in November 1947.

So it was to Platform 12 of Waterloo Station that at approximately 4.30 pm on 29th July the Prince and Princess of Wales made their way in an open carriage festooned with silver and blue balloons, and carrying astern the notice "Just Married" adorned with hearts and arrows, all hastily scrawled by Prince Andrew and Prince Edward. The bride and groom left Buckingham Palace to a Royal Salute from the Trumpeters of the Blues and Royals and to showers of rose petals, rice and other confetti from what Queen Victoria would have called "the Royal mob" who followed them to the gates of the Palace. The Princess wore a trim, short-sleeved, two-piece outfit in soft canteloupe pink, designed by the 15-year-old partnership of Belinda Belleville and David Sassoon, with an eye-catching John Boyd straw hat trimmed with ostrich feather. The crowds who lined the streets almost as thickly as earlier in the day were thrilled to see her looking confident and serene as she waved happily right and left. The carriage was a little late arriving at the station, but the honeymoon special waited. Lord Maclean was there to say his farewells, and his impeccable organisation of the day's events was rewarded by a big kiss planted firmly on his cheek by the Princess and

words of heartfelt thanks from the Prince. With that, they entered the middle coach of the three-carriage electric locomotive with its C and D logo on front and back, and bearing the name "Broadlands".

They were not quite at Broadlands yet. Just over an hour later, they reached Romsey where

they had to run the gauntlet of yet more enthusiastic crowds—this time children noticeably predominated—waiting to greet them and watch their final public progress of the day. Eventually they were within sight of the Mountbatten estate: with great difficulty they passed through the last of the throng, and as the great gate of the 6,000 acre parkland closed behind them they were alone at last. The noise of the crowds dimmed into the distance, precautions had been taken to ensure that no aircraft flew over the estate under 3,000 feet, security measures had been taken to guard against unwanted intruders, whether tourist of journalist, and the royal couple could now, for the first time, feel that the place and the moment was theirs.

Cardiff honoured its royal visitors at a reception at City Hall on 29th October. The occasion was almost emotional as the Princess received the Freedom of the City and spoke a few appreciative words in Welsh in her speech of acceptance. Outside again, she received yet more flowers, *opposite,* a further token of esteem which had become mutual in the course of the three-day tour. She hoped she would soon be back and that the parting, *below,* would be temporary.

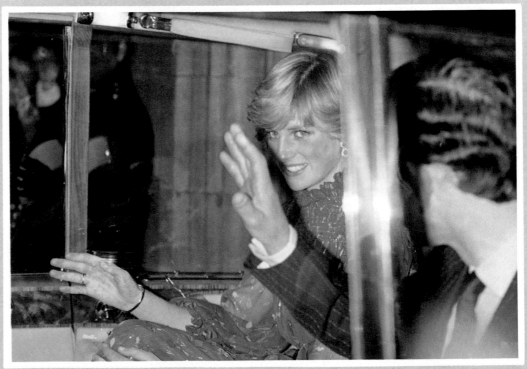

After two days' relaxation, during which Prince Charles is alleged to have gone off on his own to fish for salmon in the River Test which runs through the estate, the Prince and Princess were driven to Eastleigh airport, near Southampton, to board an RAF Andover of the Queen's Flight for Gibraltar. Their appearance at the airport was brief, almost perfunctory, and thousands who had gathered to see them were not excessively rewarded for their patience. The Prince himself piloted the aircraft for the three-hour flight and, with the Spanish authorities and Press still boiling with indignation over what was considered a calculated provocation by the Foreign Office, took great care not to fly through Spanish airspace.

When the plane touched down at Gibraltar airport, it seemed that the whole of the 30,000 population of the island must have turned out to welcome their very short-stay guests. The Rock

The flowers were probably for the Princess, *right,* **so the** Prince passed them on. The third day of the tour was much like the others: a rapturous reception everywhere, *overleaf,* with children the centre of the Princess' attention.

was alive with red, white and blue and with slogans not recommended for Spanish eyes. The visitors were welcomed at Government House by the Governor Sir William Jackson and his wife and after a forty-minute drive through a Union Jack-bedecked Main Street in an open Triumph Stag car borrowed for the occasion, and to unbridled acclamation which visibly moved them both, they finally arrived at the naval dockyard. After the usual formalities, and to the strains of the quayside orchestra playing a

selection of maritime music, they boarded the Royal Yacht Britannia for a destination known only to her crew of forty and her two august passengers. It seemed that everyone was determined to discover it, however, so thick was the traffic of boats, yachts, tugs and the like which followed the great ship out to sea.

As it was, most of them were content to pursue the Yacht no further than necessary to offer a respectful farewell. Only the Press was hot on the trail, with many ploys at the ready in order to anticipate the Yacht's route and the possible landing points: some organisations had hired ships and aircraft to go in search of the royal couple, and another elaborate network had been established whereby ships conducting their normal commercial business in the Mediterranean would report back any chance sighting of Britannia so that photographers might be transported to the area. But there were no known untoward incidents: the only event of note was the innocuous greeting offered by the Italian frigate Saggitario, which drew up alongside Britannia in the Ionian Sea and paraded its 200 crew on her bridge to give the Prince and Princess three cheers.

It was therefore with the greatest possible privacy that the royal couple were able to visit and enjoy such islands of profound legendary significance as Ithaca, Cephalonia, Kythira and Santorini, touring their ancient sites and volcanic craters as well as diving, swimming and windsurfing in those ideal conditions and idyllic surroundings.

On 12th August, Britannia reached Egypt, where the Prince and Princess were due to meet President Sadat and his wife, great personal friends of several members of the British Royal Family. In the light of events only seven weeks later, this visit which was conceived as a private one and executed with the minimum of publicity had a significance and poignancy of its own. After his assassination in early October, the President was to receive the supreme posthumous honour of the presence of his friend and heir to the British Throne at his funeral. For the moment, however, all was joy and celebration as the President welcomed the Prince and Princess onto Egyptian soil, and took them to Cairo as his guests. The couple returned the compliment the following day, when the President and Madame Sadat were entertained to dinner on board

Britannia, and it was in their presence that, amid affectionate farewells, the Prince and Princess took their leave of Egypt at Hurghada. With that, and after two weeks of almost uninterrupted sunshine—conveniently it was one of the consistently hottest spells in Europe that summer— the honeymooners were now on their way home.

And home for the time being was Balmoral, that retreat in the Highlands rebuilt by the Prince Consort, maintained long after his death in the affections of Queen Victoria and all her successors, and now warmly approved of by the Princess of Wales as "one of the best places in the world." The Queen, the Duke of Edinburgh

and Prince Charles' two brothers were already there, and it was not long before Prince Charles and his bride settled into the long-established royal holiday routine, punctuated by Sunday attendances at the little church at Crathie for Divine Service and highlighted by the annual visit to the Braemar Games in early September. For this, the Prince wore a Gordon Highlander kilt, while the Princess tactfully acknowledged the emphatic Scottishness of the occasion by

Opposite, **the smile of a** Princess whose popularity proclaimed itself throughout South Wales. *This page,* Prince Charles meets local Boy Scouts; the Princess talks to the lucky few who caught her eye—and receives this huge cuddly toy. *Overleaf,* telling studies of the Prince and Princess of Wales' informal approach.

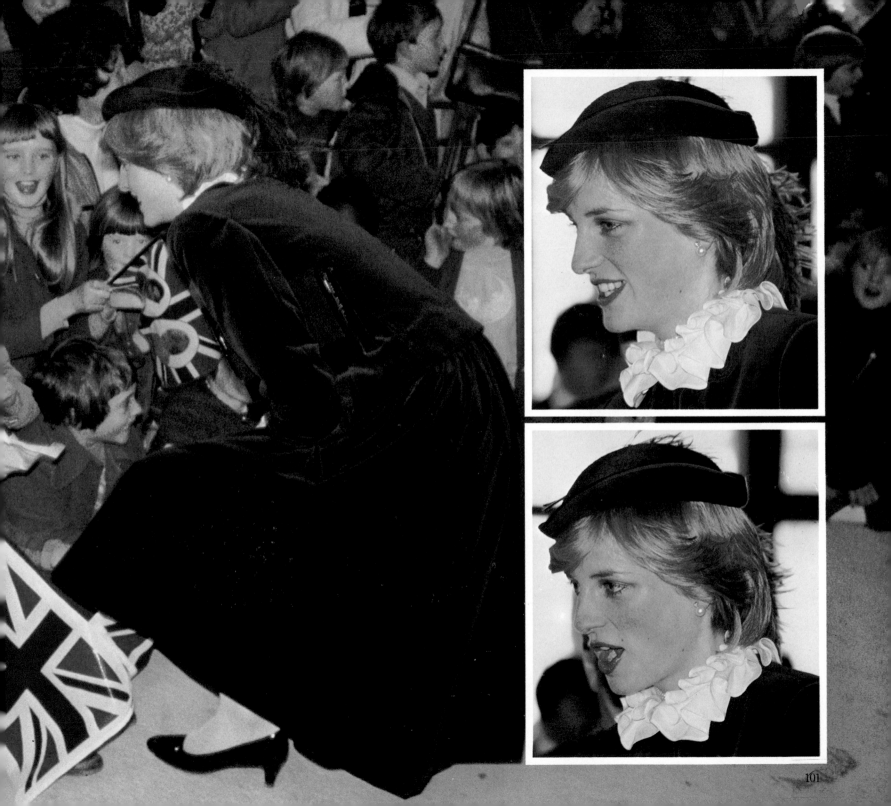

101

Right, the message on the faces of these women, who probably remembered the visit to South Wales of a previous Prince of Wales, is unmistakable. *Below,* usually those at the front attract the royal attention, but the Princess is also quick to spot another welcoming face in the thick of the crowd. *Opposite page,* a set of photographs showing the Princess' lively reactions to her meetings with the people and the dashing effect of her fashionable Belleville-Sassoon hat and high ruffle. *Overleaf,* a last handshake from Prince Charles, then he and his wife are off in the royal Rolls on a dash to the next port of call. With the gifts from the previous town packed into the back of the car, the royal couple take a quick look at the programme for the next part of the tour.

first public engagements together as man and wife. Amongst these occasional visits was one by the Princess, using the unimaginative and even suspicious alias of Mrs Smith, to the exhibition of Royal Wedding gifts at St James's Palace. This massive exhibition, which opened in the week following the wedding and remained open for a total of 525 hours during the ensuing two months consisted of about 1,200 of the couple's 6,000 gifts. Some could not be shown, such as the imaginative present of two Jersey cows, or the solid stone table offered by King Sobhuza of Swaziland, or the swimming pool for Highgrove, which was to be contructed as a gift from the Army. Other gifts, such as a holding of shares in an American oil-well and a tract of land in Bangladesh had to be refused, while others, like bicycles and pool tables, were redirected to youth clubs and organisations for the underprivileged. Those presents which were on show certainly illustrated a vast range of originality, ingenuity, wealth or personal industry on the part of the donors. At one end of the scale were a waste paper basket, half-a-dozen clothes pegs, a pair of toothbrushes, a bag of coffee beans and a hand-knitted teacosy: at the

wearing a Tam O'Shanter with her warm dark plaid outfit. The one other semi-public occasion at which the royal couple could be seen was the camera call held within a week after their arrival back in Scotland, in the hope that the Press would be sufficiently satiated with pictures that they would leave the Prince and Princess in peace for the rest of their honeymoon. It was certainly a happy interlude as the couple posed for photographs at the Brig o' Dee,

the Prince putting on his Goon act, and the Princess looking suntanned and confident, gently twitting the seventy or so cameramen as they vied for the best pictures, and voicing her unqualified approval of married life, which she highly recommended.

Both the Prince and Princess made the occasional trip away from Balmoral between the end of August and the end of October when they ended their honeymoon and performed their

other end was the fabulous collection of diamonds and sapphire jewellery, said to be worth three quarters of a million pounds, given by the Crown Prince of Saudi-Arabia, a grand piano given by the manufacturers Broadwood, the Steuben bowl acquired, it was said at bargain price, by Mrs Reagan, a brass Buddha from the King of Nepal and several prints, drawings, paintings, and statuettes. The Princess' wedding dress, together with one of the bridesmaids' dresses and a page's outfit, was also on show and it was therefore little wonder that on the first day some 6,000 people stood and queued in London's hottest weather of the year in an attempt to see these unique exhibits. Only 4,000 managed to get in on that day, but that did not discourage thousands of others from long hours of waiting for days and weeks afterwards.

Closer to the couple's new home at Highgrove, their eighteenth-century mansion in the heart of Gloucestershire, more presents were being organised. Villagers at Highgrove took one look at the dustbin that was put out every week, decided it was too tatty for the new incumbents and clubbed together to buy a new one. Not to be outdone, the citizens of Tetbury, the nearest town to Highgrove, and already the subject of a visit by the royal couple before their marriage, set up an appeal fund to buy two pairs of new gates for the house. News of the appeal reached America and funds began to come in from there. Eventually some £2,600 was collected and the gates were duly ordered. The sooner the better, as it turned out, for in August a young German woman was discovered in the grounds, apparently pining for the Prince with whom she had fallen at least as much in love as her rival the Princess!

It was cheering to see from the reports, the photographs and the couple's own remarks, that their happiness was complete. For a time both Press and public revelled in the obvious success of the match. But it was not long before the newpapers began to get wind of stories which, when published, cast shadows on the Prince and Princess' contentment. There was the gentle criticism from a Dr Laurence, Vice Chairman of the Derbyshire Area Health Authority, who chided the Princess for not eating breakfast (an admission which she had made a week or so before) and recommended that she should take "some cereal with a little bran; tea or coffee with milk; and a slice of bread." More spectacularly, the new portrait of the Princess, painted by Mr Bryan Organ after the same fashion as his earlier portrait of the Prince, was violently slashed and seriously damaged by a young student as it hung in the National Portrait Gallery in London. The student was sentenced to six months' imprisonment, and was ordered to pay £1,000 compensation towards repair work. In the event it took a total of about 250 hours of skilled labour to

restore the painting which was back in place, wisely set behind a protective shield of Perspex, by the end of November. Another untoward incident, this time in the more doubtful world of art, concerned paintings purporting to show the Princess of Wales in the nude: these were displayed in the Rotherham public house of Mr Brian Williams, but in spite of the furore it caused, the police decided not to bring any charges against him.

But these were small matters compared with the story which burst into the headlines in mid-September. All was evidently not well at home, and reports of the Princess' inability to adapt to the royal life-style—even on holiday!—began to appear. She was apparently becoming restless under the pressure of formality at Balmoral, and had wanted to move into smaller premises as soon as the Queen left for London. There were also stories that the Queen had wanted to give the Princess a gun-dog for a present, but that the Princess had refused it because of her dislike of blood sports; that she

detail: it merely denied the story of the move to smaller quarters by explaining that a decision was taken even before the wedding that, when the Queen moved back to London, the Prince and Princess would go to live at Craigowan House so that the Castle could be closed up for the winter and the servants be sent back to London. And it was left at that.

The rumours about the Princess not accompanying the royal party on shooting expeditions were contradicted in October by fresh and more damaging allegations from the League Against Cruel Sports that she had in fact shot and killed a deer, though none too cleanly, whilst on a deer-stalking outing the previous week. This led to an immediate outcry and public discussion, during which it was also alleged that the Queen was a regular deer hunter with a practised aim. As far as the Princess' activities were concerned, the Palace offered an awkwardly worded denial whose ambiguity only added fuel to the League's indignation and protest against the Princess' support for what it called "this killing

had also refused to attend the frequent shooting parties at Balmoral; that she was bored and tired by the over-long formal dinner parties there, and that she could not get used to the manner in which one should properly treat servants. Against this sort of rumour, so private in its nature, the Palace could not begin to reply in any

for fun brigade which is destroying Britain's wildlife." These major criticisms and stories, and the adverse publicity they engendered, caused the Princess considerable distress, which could hardly have been alleviated by the suggestion that she should take a portable stereo cassette player with her on shoots, so that

For the royal visit to Llwynpia Hospital the rain came down again but the crowds waited with patience and even cheerfulness beneath serried ranks of colourful umbrellas, *overleaf*. The Prince and Princess toured the maternity wing of the hospital and took what many considered an unusually close interest in the newly confined mothers and their babies. Nobody dared anticipate the news which broke the following week, although the nursing staff later admitted to having watched for any tell-tale signs of the Princess' pregnancy.

she could be near her husband without being obliged to hear the constant blast of the guns. Notwithstanding, she continued to make brief public appearances, showing no sign of disillusion or worry, and her surprise visit to London to see all her former pupils and colleagues at the Young England Kindergarten was a delightful reminder, for her and for them, of the relatively carefree days before she became a fully fledged member of the Royal Family.

By this time the bomb threats which preceded the Welsh tour were forgotten, and appropriately enough the Princess was carrying not only flowers but also a Welsh flag. Meanwhile, Prince Charles was able to conduct his own walkabout, *opposite centre left*, as his wife busied herself with those endless crowds of children.

On 27th October the Prince and Princess of Wales, long honeymoon ended, and they began their lifetime's round of public service together with a three-day tour of Wales. It required no strain on the imagination to discover why Wales had been chosen as the background to the beginning of this new chapter in their lives: Prince Charles had, since his Investiture in 1969, devoted much of his official and some of his private time to the welfare of the Principality of which he is the titular head, and his decision to

bring his wife to his subjects at the very outset of their public career was a statement of his continuing concern to adduce reality and purpose to the fact of his constitutional links with them. There was doubtless an element of goodwill too, in the face of the Welsh Nationalist minorities who had, at least since the Investiture been a force to reckon with and were again back in the news with schemes to upset plans for the tour. Huge security operations became indispensible as the first day of the visit approached: the whereabouts of known extremists were checked, buildings bordering the royal routes were scrutinised, and last minute thorough searches took place after an incendiary device was found at Pontypridd. The tour itself was not without its ration of protest

Previous page and these pages, **the Prince and Princess** of Wales attending a gala concert at Brangwen Hall, Swansea on 28th October. *Overleaf,* back in London, they went with the Queen to the State Opening of Parliament at Westminster on 4th November.

incidents—anti-royalist or anti-English banners, hostile shouting and chanting *en masse*, stink bombs and the spraying of the royal car with aerosol paint—but overall the whirlwind programme incorporating over a dozen towns and every county was a resounding success.

The Princess of Wales was of course the person everyone came to see, and on the first day she tactfully wore an outfit of very Welsh design and in the equally Welsh colours of red and green. In spite of the bitterly cold weather, thousands of people waited long hours to greet her and they were well rewarded as she spent much of her time on walkabouts, talking to children and shaking hands with their mothers.

On one occasion she stopped to embrace a child suffering from spina bifida who was drawn up to the front of the crowd in a wheelchair. Later on at Rhyl she was asked by a 7-year-old boy if he could give her a kiss too—she said yes, so he did. Also in line for a kiss was Lord Snowdon who, as Constable of Caernarvon Castle, greeted his nephew and new niece as they arrived to visit the site of Prince Charles' Investiture.

On the second day it was the turn of South-West Wales to welcome the royal couple. This time the weather was thoroughly unwelcoming with heavy and persistent rain to accompany the dismal cold. But again, spirits remained high. The tone of indifference to the weather was set

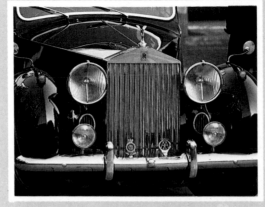

Opposite page, left, **the Princess of Wales, resplendent in an** evening dress which matched the glories of the exhibition "Splendours of the Gonzaga" at which she was present on 4th November. The following day, Buckingham Palace announced that she was expecting her first child, and the Prince and Princess went to London's Guildhall for lunch with the Lord Mayor, Sir Ronald Gardner-Thorpe. The memory of the couple's wedding and the anticipation of their parenthood was neatly linked by the Lord Mayor in his speech of welcome. *Opposite right,* the arrival at the Guildhall, and, *this page,* the departure.

by the Princess herself, whose dashing ostrich-feather hat became bedraggled and cloying as she continued her walkabouts in the rain regardless of personal comfort. Prince Charles, who was a solicitous husband throughout the tour, eventually persuaded her to use an umbrella. Much to the cynicism of Welsh Nationalists, the Princess had learned a few words of Welsh, and was able to say "Diolch yn fawr" (Thank you very

much) as she received numerous gifts of flowers, Welsh dolls and posies from people in the crowds. At St David's they both attended a service of thanksgiving to commemorate the 800th anniversary of the Cathedral, with Prince Charles reading the lesson in English and Welsh. There was, however, an embarrassing moment when the Princess' Welsh utterly failed her: at one point in the service "Land of My Fathers" was sung in Welsh, and while the Prince sang lustily, the Princess bowed her head apologetically and almost ashamedly. But embarrassment was soon forgotten as, ten minutes behind schedule, the couple visited Haverfordwest, where they mingled freely with the crowds, paying special attention to a group of mentally handicapped people. Then on to Carmarthen where crowds six deep waved and cheered in the appalling weather: the rain sheeted down, the water poured down the streets and slopped over the shoes of the royal visitors.

It was clear by now that the couple, and the Princess in particular, had taken the Pricipality by storm. On the third day there was more rain at Pontypridd but the demonstrations of public affection for the couple was greater than ever, as if its citizens were striving to outdo the welcomes received in previous towns. At Builth Wells, the Prince and Princess visited an agricultural showground and were given a Welsh Black heifer and a Welsh Mountain ewe for their farm at Highgrove. In the Rhondda Valley they opened the maternity wing of Llwynpia Hospital where the Princess indulged in baby talk with expectant and nursing mothers. The Prince was no less interested, and during a conversation with one mother, let slip his approval of the idea of husbands being present at the birth of their children. "I'm sure that's a very good thing," he said—then, seeing the television cameras and

eyeing the reporters, wryly added, "I expect I shall get a lot of letters about that." Little did we suspect what the following week would bring!

Eventually the couple arrived at Cardiff where an ecstatic crowd gathered to see them open a huge recreation and community complex. They completed their tour with a ceremony at the City Hall Cardiff, in which the Princess received the freedom of the city to a heartwarming standing ovation. The ceremony was as impressive and charged with fervour as the Princess' words of thanks were simple: "I realise it is a great honour. I am glad to be Princess of such a wonderful place." She hoped that she would be able to pay future visits to Wales, and that she would be able to speak more Welsh by then. At that point it seemed as if a second visit could not be far away; the goodwill engendered by the huge, uniformly affectionate crowds and by the visitors they all came to cheer, was testimony to the fact that, even in this hard-pressed Principality, the magic of the monarchy had been successfully worked again.

The Prince and Princess returned triumphant from this exacting whistle-stop tour to London, where more sedate duties awaited them. Prince Charles' long association with the arts—a department in which his wife has yet to indicate her own tastes—brought three engagements in rapid succession in early November. On the 1st they visited Blenheim Palace to attend an English Heritage concert. On the 3rd they were guests of honour at the splendid gala opening of the 25th National Film Festival at the National Film Institute on the South Bank. The next day they were at the Victoria and Albert Museum in Kensington where they opened the sumptuous exhibition "Splendours of the Gonzaga"—a history in art and music of the extravagant and magnificent way in which the Gonzaga family elevated and monopolised the old Renaissance city state of Mantua for three centuries. The

Commemoration time again as the Prince and Princess of Wales planted two saplings in Hyde Park to commemorate their wedding and the forthcoming birth of their child. The Princess sported the same tartan outfit she wore at Braemar. *Overleaf,* at the beginning of the next week she joined the Queen Mother, Princess Alice and King Olav of Norway to watch the Queen, Prince Philip, Prince Charles, the Duke of Kent and Prince Michael lay wreaths at the Cenotaph on Remembrance Sunday. *Following pages,* visits to Chesterfield and, *right,* York followed on 12th November, between bouts of morning sickness which curtailed the Princess' activities during the following weeks.

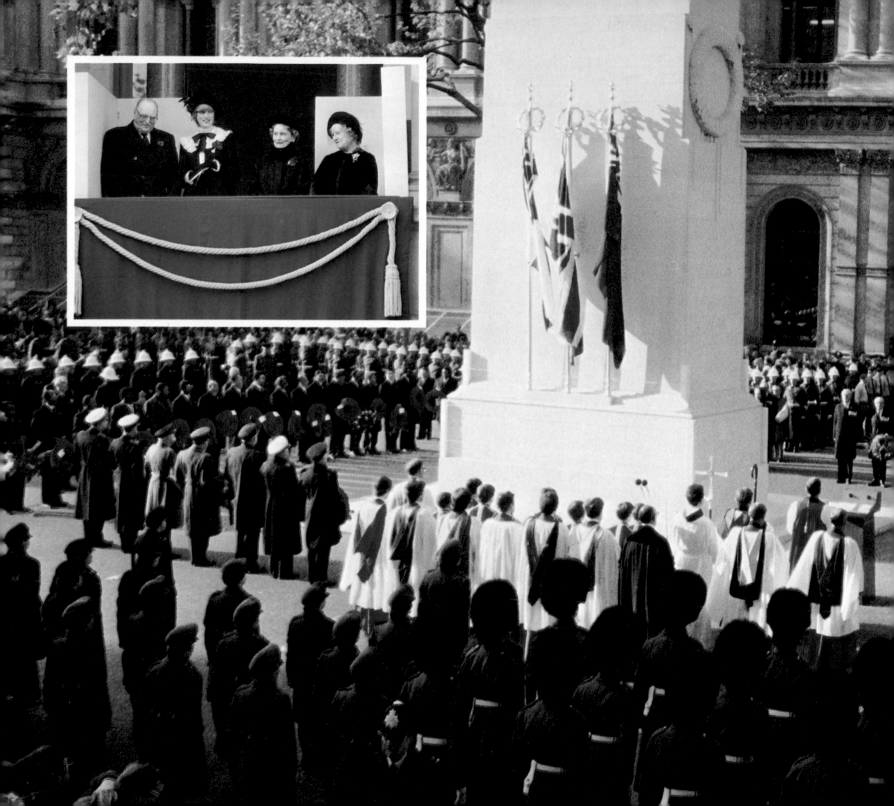

grandeur of the story was matched by the high tone of the opening ceremony with 700 guests present, many from Italy, in addition to the Prince and Princess. The Princess wore another of her celebrated off-the-shoulder gowns, this time in shimmering white, perfectly suited to the splendour of the history which surrounded her. The Prince was in jocular mood: addressing the guests during the opening, he spotted a couple of Raphael cartoons on the wall and threatened to have them removed to hang at Highgrove, since they had only been lent to the Museum by Queen Victoria. It was that kind of an evening— formal in concept but leavened by that delightful brand of informality with which the Prince is so adept at investing such occasions, and to which the Princess equally applied herself, laughing

Late in November the Princess of Wales carried out her first solo engagement when, "without my better half", she switched on the Christmas lights in London's Regent Street. Typically, she said she was pleased for the children, who looked forward to the lights each year.

freely when her husband forgot his lines during his speech, and talking avidly with her hosts about various items in the exhibition which, overall, she found "gorgeous."

Earlier that day she had accompanied Prince Charles, for the first momentous time, to the State Opening of Parliament. In most years this is the most splendid occasion in the Queen's autumn programme: a totally ceremonial function attended not only by royalty in its most glittering guise, but by fully robed members of the House of Lords, the titled judiciary in their

full-bottomed wigs, and by the vast senior diplomatic complement of London's foreign embassies with their wives gowned and tiara'd or in national dress. This time, the Queen, opening Parliament in this thirtieth year of her reign, was accompanied on the steps of the Throne by the largest family contingent ever. The Duke of Edinburgh was on her left as usual, and to his left were Princess Anne and Captain Phillips. On the Queen's right sat the Prince of Wales, a seasoned attender since October 1967. On his right sat the Princess of Wales, looking very much on her debut, and wearing a dress of the simplest design and in purest white as if deliberately trying to avoid drawing attention to herself as a possible competitor for the attentions of those present. It was, however, inevitable that she should be watched very carefully by those looking for signs of nervousness or waiting for the wrong move, but the Princess did not oblige, rising perfectly to the occasion and taking it all in her stride. Perhaps she had already acquired the knack of adapting to the rules of the royal game. Perhaps on the other hand she was terribly preoccupied with the matter which next day would make national and international news.

It was Thursday 5th November, just three months after that superlative wedding which in happier times would have qualified 1981 for the title *annus mirabilis.* At 11 o'clock that morning Buckingham Palace announced that "the Princess of Wales is expecting a baby next June." The crisp, bald statement took just about everyone by surprise. Quite apart from the fact that few had got over the vivid memory of the royal wedding and had not therefore begun to think of the Prince and Princess in the context of parents, there was every justification for not expecting them to start a family quite as early as they had obviously intended. The Princess' youth had something to do with it: despite her mature bearing, she was still only 20—an age which many young women regard as too young to be giving up the pleasures of comparative freedom for the demands and responsibilities of parenthood. In addition, her high-speed introduction into the specialised world of the Royal family has thus far been at best basic, and although many types of duties were covered, many others were left unexplored. Among these were the royal tours abroad, and indeed the couple's prospective visits in 1982 to Australia, New Zealand and Canada had to be postponed as soon as the announcement was made.

In the light of events, however, we may now reflect that other considerations might have been stronger. The Princess' abiding love of children is now almost taken for granted, and the prospect of having her own was probably one she was unwilling to wait for. It was instructive that, after the announcement, the Princess' former flatmates averred that they were not surprised by the news. For his part, Prince Charles, then almost 33, would equally understandably not want to endure the experience of public (and possibly family) pressure on him to produce children, particularly with the

On 21st December the Prince and Princess of Wales visited Guildford Cathedral to attend a Christmas celebration organised by the Surrey region of the Prince's Trust. This charity, of which Prince Charles is President, seeks to give help by providing advice, facilities or cash to groups of young people wanting to improve their social amenities. Again, the crowd's patient waiting in the snow was amply rewarded.

memory fresh in his mind of the prolonged and sometimes heavy pressure he had had to tolerate from those who thought he ought to be married. Additionally one should take into account the more general, if emotionally nebulous, concern to produce a further direct heir to the Throne—a materialistic rather than spiritual desire, but inevitable given the strong dynastic

nature of the institution of which he was part.

However this may be there was no mistaking the universal delight when the news of the Princess' early pregnancy was received. Naturally the family was pleased—the announcement said so, adding that "the Queen was personally informed of the news some days ago." The Princess' father, Earl Spencer, could not sufficiently express his pleasure but intimated how much his daughter had wanted a baby and said what a marvellous mother she would make.

Studies of the Princess of Wales taken inside Guildford Cathedral as she met officials of the Prince's Trust. By now, the bouts of illness which caused her to cancel earlier engagements were over and she radiated serenity and happiness as these pictures show. It was good to hear that she would continue with her duties well into 1982.

Her mother, Mrs Shand Kydd, said it was "wonderful news" and hinted that she might just bend her own teetotal rules to celebrate it. And Barbara Cartland, the Princess' self confessed eccentric "step" grandmother, cooed contentedly, musing over the success of the love match and looking forward to the beautiful baby which, she said, was always the result of a pregnancy conceived between two people truly in love. This sentiment was echoed by Harold Brooks-Baker of Debrett, who anticipated the

and speculation. At Highgrove there was effusive gratification and one of the villagers said there was now much more purpose behind the bonfire parties which that evening would bring. At Tetbury, the Mayor left his office and walked to the Market Square to drink champagne beneath the Union Jack, and was joined by celebrating townspeople.

Meanwhile the objects of the morning's praise and admiration were their way to the Guildhall

emergence of "new Royal genes of excellence."

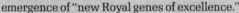

Outside the family circle interest and enthralment were scarcely less intense. Spectators of the Changing of the Guard outside the Palace were, if they were foreigners, bowled over by the news, whilst the more phlegmatic Londoners nodded thoughtfully and with evident inner satisfaction. For many of them Prince Charles had suddenly become something of a hero while his wife had all but assumed the classical and even Biblical virtues with which the name Diana is associated. The Queen held one of her luncheon parties that day, and the guests noticed how very relaxed and contented she seemed, looking "definintely at peace with the world as everyone offered their congratulations." Further afield, radio and television were soon carrying the news and households and villages up and down the country buzzed with reminiscence

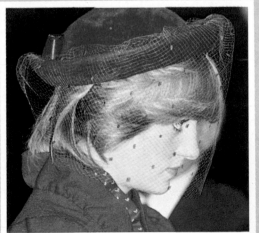

130

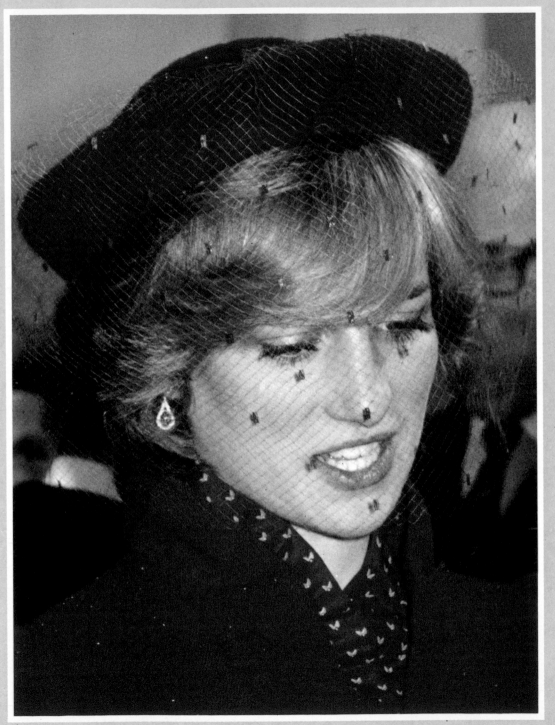

for a Mayoral luncheon. The announcement brought thousands of City workers away from their own lunches and onto the streets to give the couple a noisy reception replete with congratulation and good wishes. The welcome inside the Guildhall, if more formal, lost nothing in enthusiasm, and the after-luncheon speeches gave Prince Charles the opportunity publicly to express how much he appreciated the unique atmosphere of affection and support which he and his wife experienced at the time of their wedding: "It was extraordinary and it made me proud to be British," he said. More important, he now felt able, in the light of all the congratulations being heaped upon the Princesss, to give tongue to the debt he owed to her: in a statement rarely rivalled for personal content as part of an official speech, he recalled the recent resounding tour of Wales and attributed the people's response "entirely to the effect my dear wife has had on everybody."

There was no indication from either the Prince or Princess—or indeed from any other source—that any significant decision had been taken, or even considered, about the baby or the circumstances of its expected birth. No royal preferences as to its sex were confessed; indeed, the Princess, in reply to such an enquiry while on tour later that month, gave the classic answer: "I don't mind whether it's a boy or girl so long as it's healthy." And while its sex remains necessarily undisclosed the choice of a name (or rather names) must remain a gamble. A boy, with his claim to, the Crown after his father, will almost certainly be given a traditional royal name, most likely that of a former king. George is a strong possibility, in honour of the grandfather Prince Charles admires but barely remembers, and of the much maligned monarch, George III, whose reputation Prince Charles has done much

After arriving at Guildford Cathedral, *opposite page,* and meeting their hosts, *above,* Prince Charles and his wife were asked to cut a Christmas cake, *right.* They took the point when one of the local branch officers was heard to whisper: "I bet this takes you back!"

to bring into balance. James is another likely name, extending as it would the precedent for Stuart names set by the Queen at the births of Prince Charles in 1948 and Princess Anne in 1950. It would also please the Scots to see the possibility of a Scots name back among the list of Kings and Queens for the first time since 1688. It

The service and celebration over, the Prince and Princess made their way out into the snow again to meet those who had waited for another chance to see them on this their last public engagement before the Christmas and New Year break at Windsor and Sandringham. That in the face of such inclement weather, the crowds did not diminish as the evening wore on is testimony to the immense popularity that the Prince and Princess have established and maintained in one of the busiest years they will ever spend together.

would be surprising if one of a male child's subsidiary names were not Louis, as Prince Charles rarely misses an opportunity to honour the memory of Lord Mountbatten, while other close family names—Charles, Philip, Andrew, Edward, John (after Lord Spencer), recommend themselves at least as strongly as the standard Welsh name David.

In the case of a girl, since the chances of her ascending the Throne are more remote while the convention of male primogeniture persists, the choice of names is in effect much greater and may easily embrace those not having the established royal imprimatur of traditional usage. While, therefore, Elizabeth and Victoria must on the strength of precedent remain firm favourites, there is ample scope for innovation by the introduction of names from the Princess' own family—Diana, Frances, Sarah, Jane, Ruth—and it is widely imagined that the Princess' untrammelled approach to her duties will be reflected in the choice of names for her child.

The other main question arising in the wake of the official announcement was that of where the birth would take place. Until the late 1960s it was customary for royal babies to be born within the royal homes, official or private—Prince Charles, Prince Andrew and Prince Edward were born at Buckingham Palace, Princess Anne and Viscount Linley at Clarence House. In the 1970s, however, the tendency was for royal mothers-to-be to go to hospital for their confinements—since 1969 the Duchesses of Kent and Gloucester and Princess Anne and Princess

Michael have given birth to their children in hospital. And by far the most favoured choice has been the Lindo Wing of St Mary's Hospital Paddington, tucked almost remotely away from the once favoured royal households. It seems almost a travesty of tradition that a possible future sovereign should be born in hospital— even in a £2,000 bed in the private wing—and

somehow it is difficult to envisage Prince Charles' sense of precedent allowing such a thing to happen. But when on the other hand one considered that the Queen herself can boast a birthplace with no more prepossessing an address than 17 Bruton Street (the London home of her maternal grandparents), it is perfectly conceivable that the generally accepted arrangement by which potential heirs to the British

Above **Christmas Day 1981: the Princess of Wales with Princes Edward, Andrew and Charles after Morning Service at St George's Chapel, Windsor.** *Other pictures and overleaf* the Prince and Princess of Wales at a fair at Tulse Hill on 23rd January. They met stallholders and organisers, and the Princess even found time to retrieve a photographer's lens.

Crown are born within its palaces will shortly be discontinued as out-of-date and impracticable.

The euphoria over the Princess of Wales' pregnancy quickly subsided as, within four days of it, she was obliged to start cancelling visits. Morning sickness had set in almost coincidentally with the date of the announcement, and a two-day tour of Duchy of Cornwall estates in the South-West became the first casualty. The Prince went on his own and was beseiged by reporters eager for details as if they had no inkling of what the reason for the Princess' absence could be. His reply was casual and authoritative: "You all have wives: you all know the problems." Nevertheless, the Duchy tenants were disappointed that they were unable to see and congratulate the Princess personally, and at the prospect of such a long wait before they might see her again. The citizens of York and Chesterfield were luckier: she was able to keep to the full programme of a busy day of engagements on 12th November. At York she was

showered with not only flowers but also gifts of baby clothes and toys, in such number that they all had to be passed back to her lady-in-waiting and then to policemen and women who had a difficult time keeping up with the pressure. She

won warm applause for being sporting enough to travel on a model of Stephenson's steam locomotive "Rocket" when she and the Prince visited the Railway Museum, and all in all could have been in no doubt as to the quality of the Yorkshire welcome. At Chesterfield Prince Charles warmed to another superb reception. "We were warned about you," he said, "and it has turned out to be absolutely true."

The pace was unfortunately too swift to be maintained. Although the Princess continued in

The event at Tulse Hill was the fund-raising January Fair at the Dick Sheppard School. Informal as ever, the Princess talked to many of the children, and even won a plastic knife and fork on the Tombola stall.

excellent general health, a fact that the Palace was anxious to make clear, crowds waited in vain at Sandringham that weekend to see the Prince and Princess attend church. The Princess was not well enough to attend even this comparatively undemanding event, and there were rumours that she spent the whole day in bed feeling wretched. On 18th November, Prince Charles went alone to Bristol as the Palace explained that the stamina necessary for long day visits and walkabouts in large towns and cities was beyond the Princess' medical advice. Prince Charles was quick to assure everyone that there was nothing more in it than that, and that the Princess' absences were merely the result of sensible precautions. He added, almost boastfully that he was "quite prepared to take full responsibility for her situation." The Princess cancelled a futher visit to the South West—this time to Falmouth—on 1st December, and maintained a comparatively low profile until Christmas and the New Year took the whole of the Royal Family away from public engagements for five weeks. The Princess did, however, consent to officiate at the switching on of the Christmas lights in Regent Street—her first solo engagement, and to attend with Prince Charles a beautiful carol service in Guildford Cathedral in aid of the Prince's Trust for disadvantaged children.

The resumption by the Prince and Princess of Wales of duties on a more regular basis in January brought them almost full circle to the first anniversary of their engagement. History will lend credibility to the fact, but at present it is almost unbelievable that the roving, sporting Prince who at one time seemed almost content with his bachelor existence, should in so short a time have been made his decision to marry, acted upon it and now be facing the prospect of fatherhood. Equally it seems less than real that from that coy, unassuming unknown quantity Lady Diana Spencer, we should within the year have the good fortune to see emerge a self-assured and capable Princess of Wales with her good humour, sensible approachability and infectious delight in the company of the young—all attributes enjoyed in generous measure. One may be forgiven for thinking that the events in which they have both featured have in the last twelve months been almost too hectic to assimilate, but by the same token it is worth reflecting that the period has been one of enduring happiness for our Royal Family and of great potential for the monarchy it represents and serves. That potential resides in the happy and compatible couple whose joys their future subjects have been privileged to observe and, from

not too great a distance, share. The same potential is symbolised by the infant whose birth is now eagerly awaited as an event of hope and regeneration in the continuing process and development of hereditary rule.

While touring the January Fair at the Dick Sheppard School, the Princess received a huge teddy bear from eight-year-old Sarah Broadbent, and learned a little more about the art of holding a baby when she took 14-month-old Kate O'Flaherty in her arms. This was the first of a limited number of engagements to be undertaken by the Princess until early April, when she will prepare in earnest for the birth of her own baby.

TEXT BY
TREVOR HALL
Designed by Philip Clucas MSIAD

**Produced by Ted Smart
and David Gibbon**

First published in Great Britain 1982 by
Colour Library International Ltd.
©1982 Illustrations and text:
Colour Library International Ltd.,
New Malden, Surrey, England
Colour separations by
FERCROM, Barcelona, Spain
Display and text filmsetting by
Focus Photoset and The Printed Word,
London, England
Printed and bound in Barcelona, Spain
by JISA-RIEUSSET & EUROBINDER

ISBN 0 906558 96 4

COLOUR LIBRARY INTERNATIONAL

D.L.B. 5178